S0-BXY-475

SCI
7

Mathematical Models in Linguistics

PRENTICE-HALL FOUNDATIONS OF MODERN LINGUISTICS SERIES

Sanford A. Schane
editor

John Kimball   Formal Theory of Grammar

Robert P. Stockwell   Foundations of Syntactic Theory

Sanford A. Schane   Generative Phonology

Maurice Gross   Mathematical Models in Linguistics

William S-Y. Wang   Phonetics

Janet Dean Fodor   Semantics

Suzette Haden Elgin   What is Linguistics?

Other titles to be announced

Mathematical Models in Linguistics

MAURICE GROSS

University of Paris, Vincennes

PRENTICE-HALL, INC., ENGLEWOOD CLIFFS, NEW JERSEY

© 1972 PRENTICE-HALL, INC., Englewood Cliffs, New Jersey

*All rights reserved. No part of this book
may be reproduced in any forms or by any means
without the written permission of the publisher.*

Printed in the United States of America

Library of Congress Catalog Card Number: 75-181401

ISBN: 0-13-561696-4C
0-13-561688-3P

10 9 8 7 6 5 4 3 2 1

PRENTICE-HALL INTERNATIONAL, INC., LONDON
PRENTICE-HALL OF AUSTRALIA, PTY. LTD., SYDNEY
PRENTICE-HALL OF CANADA, LTD., TORONTO
PRENTICE-HALL OF INDIA PRIVATE LIMITED, NEW DELHI
PRENTICE-HALL OF JAPAN, INC., TOKYO

Editor's Note

Language permeates human interaction, culture, behavior, and thought. The *Foundations of Modern Linguistics Series* focuses on current research in the nature of language.

Linguistics as a discipline has undergone radical change within the last decade. Questions raised by today's linguists are not necessarily those asked previously by traditional grammarians or by structural linguists. Most of the available introductory texts on linguistics, having been published several years ago, cannot be expected to portray the colorful contemporary scene. Nor is there a recent book surveying the spectrum of modern linguistic research, probably because the field is still moving too fast, and no one author can hope to capture the diverse moods reflected in the various areas of linguistic inquiry. But it does not seem unreasonable now to ask individual specialists to provide a picture of how they view their own particular field of interest. With the *Foundations of Modern Linguistic Series* we will attempt to organize the kaleidoscopic present-day scene. Teachers in search of up-to-date materials can choose individual volumes of the series for courses in linguistics and in the nature of language.

If linguistics is no longer what it was ten years ago its relation to other disciplines has also changed. Language is peculiarly human and it is found deep inside the mind. Consequently, the problems of modern linguistics are equally of concern to anthropology, sociology, psychology, and philosophy. Linguistics has always had a close affiliation with literature and with foreign language learning. Developments in other areas have had their impact on linguistics. There are mathematical models of language and formalisms of its structure. Computers are being used to test grammars. Other sophisticated instrumentation has revolutionized research in phonetics. Advances in neurology have contributed to our understanding of language pathologies and to the development of language. This series is also intended, then, to acquaint other disciplines with the progress going on in linguistics.

Finally, we return to our first statement. Language permeates our lives. We sincerely hope that the *Foundations of Modern Linguistics Series* will be of interest to anyone wanting to know what language is and how it affects us.

Sanford A. Schane, *editor*

Contents

Foreword   *xv*

The Conceptual Background   *1*

Objectives and Methods   **1.1**   *1*

STRUCTURAL LINGUISTICS   *1.1.1*   *1*
MATHEMATICAL LOGIC   *1.1.2*   *5*
COMPUTATION   *1.1.3*   *5*

Basic Mathematical Concepts   **1.2**   *8*

SETS   *1.2.1*   *8*
STRINGS   *1.2.2*   *14*
*MONOIDS   *1.2.3*   *15*
POLYNOMIALS AND SERIES ON STRINGS   *1.2.4*   *16*

Applications to Natural Languages   **1.3**   *19*

BASIC PROPERTIES OF LANGUAGES   *1.3.1*   *19*
FACTORIZATION OF STRINGS   *1.3.2*   *22*
POLYNOMIALS ON PHONEMES   *1.3.3*   *24*
A NOTATION IN PHONOLOGY   *1.3.4*   *25*

Turing Machines   *26*

Definitions   **2.1**   *26*

THE MACHINE   *2.1.1*   *26*
COMPUTATIONS   *2.1.2*   *26*
DETERMINICITY   *2.1.3*   *27*

Definition of Languages   **2.2**   *32*

CHARACTERISTIC FUNCTIONS   *2.2.1*   *32*
WEAK ACCEPTANCE   *2.2.2*   *32*
FUNDAMENTAL PROPERTIES OF LANGUAGES   *2.2.3*   *33*
REMARKS   *2.2.4*   *34*

Extensions of Turing Machines   **2.3**   *34*

UNIVERSAL TURING MACHINES   *2.3.1*   *34*
GENERALIZATIONS OF TURING MACHINES *2.3.2*   *35*

Formal Systems   *37*

Rewriting Systems   **3.1**   *37*

DEFINITIONS   *3.1.1*   *37*
REWRITING RULES AND BUILDING PROCESSES   *3.1.2*   *39*
AUXILIARY SYMBOLS   *3.1.3*   *40*
VARIABLES   *3.1.4*   *43*
EXTENSIONS OF REWRITING SYSTEMS   *3.1.5*   *45*

*Algebraic Systems   **3.2**   *46*

THE EQUIVALENCE RELATION ⟺   *3.2.1*   *46*
THE CONGRUENCE RELATION ⟺   *3.2.2*   *47*

THE PRODUCT OF CLASSES	*3.2.3*	*48*
MORPHISM	*3.2.4*	*49*
REMARKS	*3.2.5*	*51*

IV

Relations Between Turing Machines and Rewriting Systems   *51*

Turing Machines and Rewriting Systems	**4.1**	*52*
Turing Machines for Substitutions	**4.2**	*54*
Formal Systems Simulating Turing Machines	**4.3**	*56*
Flowcharts	**4.4**	*58*
Generation Versus Recognition	**4.5**	*60*

V

Computing Systems and Natural Languages   *63*

Natural Languages as Recursively Enumerable Sets	**5.1**	*63*
Special Properties of Natural Languages	**5.2**	*64*
Linguistic Motivation	**5.3**	*65*
LINGUISTIC FACTS	*5.3.1*	*65*
THE USE OF SYMBOLS	*5.3.2*	*70*
TERMINAL AND AUXILIARY VOCABULARIES	*5.3.3*	*70*
Grammar Rules	**5.4**	*73*
Rules and Computing Devices	**5.5**	*74*
DELETIONS	*5.5.1*	*74*
INSERTIONS	*5.5.2*	*76*
PERMUTATIONS	*5.5.3*	*77*

Finite State Processes   *78*

Finite Automaton	**6.1**	*78*
Other Interpretations	**6.2**	*80*
FINITE-STATE GRAPHS	*6.2.1*	*81*
PRODUCING AUTOMATON	*6.2.2*	*81*
FINITE-STATE GRAMMARS	*6.2.3*	*82*
A LANGUAGE THAT IS NOT A K-LANGUAGE	*6.2.4*	*83*
REMARKS ON INTERPRETATION	*6.2.5*	*84*
Regular Expressions	**6.3**	*85*
*Algebraic Systems Associated to a Finite Automaton	**6.4**	*87*
AUTOMATA AND MAPPINGS	*6.4.1*	*87*
THE MONOID OF AN AUTOMATON	*6.4.2*	*91*
Extensions of the Definition of Finite Automaton	**6.5**	*94*
Formal Properties of K-Languages	**6.6**	*95*
UNION	*6.6.1*	*95*
PRODUCT	*6.6.2*	*96*
STAR	*6.6.3*	*96*
Application to Syntax	**6.7**	*96*
Application to Morphophonology	**6.8**	*99*

Context-Free Languages   *100*

Constituent Analysis of Natural Languages	**7.1**	*100*
Examples of C-Grammars	**7.2**	*102*
Derivations and Trees	**7.3**	*103*

Ambiguity	**7.4**	*105*
Description of C-Grammars	**7.5**	*107*
SELF-EMBEDDING GRAMMARS	*7.5.1*	*107*
CLASSES OF C-GRAMMARS	*7.5.2*	*108*
REPRESENTATIONS OF STRUCTURES	*7.5.3*	*109*
*ALGEBRAIC EQUATIONS	*7.5.4*	*110*
A Language That Is Not a C-Language	**7.6**	*112*
Formal Properties	**7.7**	*112*
CLOSURE PROPERTIES	*7.7.1*	*113*
INTERSECTION	*7.7.2*	*114*
Push-Down Automata	**7.8**	*114*
DEFINITIONS	*7.8.1*	*115*
EQUIVALENCE WITH C-GRAMMARS	*7.8.2*	*116*
REMARKS	*7.8.3*	*118*
*Algebraic Characterization	**7.9**	*120*
DYCK LANGUAGES	*7.9.1*	*120*
ALGEBRAIC DEFINITION	*7.9.2*	*122*
EQUIVALENCE BETWEEN C-GRAMMARS AND ALGEBRAIC SYSTEM	*7.9.3*	*122*

VIII

Linguistic Adequacy of Mathematical Models

124

Natural Languages Characterized as Sets of Strings	**8.1**	*124*
NATURAL LANGUAGES AND K-LANGUAGES	*8.1.1*	*125*
NATURAL LANGUAGES AND C-LANGUAGES	*8.1.2*	*127*
Representation of Constraints	**8.2**	*129*
TREE STRUCTURES OF K-GRAMMARS	*8.2.1*	*129*
INADEQUACIES OF C-STRUCTURES	*8.2.2*	*129*
Context-Sensitive Languages	**8.3**	*132*
DEFINITIONS	*8.3.1*	*132*
OTHER FORMS OF RULES	*8.3.2*	*133*
FORMAL PROPERTIES	*8.3.3*	*135*
APPLICATIONS	*8.3.4*	*136*

Transformational Grammars   **8.4**   *140*

INADEQUACIES OF CONSTITUENT STRUCTURE   *8.4.1*   *140*
FORMALIZATION OF TRANSFORMATIONS   *8.4.2*   *143*
HARRIS' VIEW OF TRANSFORMATIONS   *8.4.3*   *151*

Conclusion   *153*

Selected Readings   *155*

Index   *157*

Foreword

Structural linguistics deals with the properties of natural languages that are best accounted for in terms of combinations of simple elements into more complex ones. For example, morphology deals with the combinations of phonemes (i.e. elementary sounds that roughly correspond to letters) into words. Syntax is concerned with the arrangement of words into sentences. These combinations are by no means arbitrary, and the main empirical task consists in discovering what they are, and under what conditions they are allowed. There exist laws that restrict them, and all linguists are pursuing one goal, discovering these laws. In the last twenty years, considerable advances have been made, and in many cases the results of linguistic research have reached a degree of precision and complexity such that the use of mathematical tools has become the only safe way to state the descriptions.

Presented here are a number of such tools, in terms of standard mathematical notations. At the same time, it is attempted, by means of general examples, to show how they are put to use in linguistics, and hopefully how they might result in the setting up of fruitful models.

Most of the devices described are also used in computer sciences in connection with the treatment of programming languages. Students of computer technology will find here a concrete interpretation of these abstract mechanisms.

The reader will find various levels of mathematical abstraction. The main body of this book is mathematical in a very elementary way: starting from empirical data, various concepts are defined, and consistent notations are used to deal with them. In a few places, more sophisticated algebraic structures are extracted from formal descriptions. For such cases the reader needs some knowledge of elementary abstract algebra, which can be found for example in R. E. Wall's *Introduction to Algebraic Linguistics* (Prentice-Hall). However, all necessary definitions have been given, so that these parts can be fully understood, but more attention will be required from the reader with only an elementary mathematical background. The corresponding paragraphs are distinguished by an asterisk (*). Omitting them will not affect the understanding of the rest of the book.

My presentation owes a great deal to the work of N. Chomsky and G. A. Miller, M. Davis, and Z. S. Harris. The comments and criticisms of M. Nivat, G. H. Matthews, M. P. Schützenberger, and R. E. Wall have greatly improved the content of this book. Special thanks go to S. Schane and D. M. Daly who suggested numerous improvements and corrected many details; T. M. Lightner and J. R. Ross helped me constantly during the 1968 Summer Linguistics Institute in Urbana, Illinois, and during my stay in the department of Linguistics at the University of Texas at Austin.

The Conceptual Background

Structural linguistics developed original methods,
but influences from logic and computer science
favored the introduction of various mathematical
techniques currently used in
transformational linguistics.

Objectives and Methods

1.1.1
STRUCTURAL LINGUISTICS

Mathematical linguistics was made possible through developments in structural linguistics, which freed the study of language from many aspects and concepts that could not be made operational. Such concepts, mainly semantic ones, led to disagreement among linguists, unscientific discussions, and the blurring of many correct reasonings about linguistic facts.

Consider the following examples taken from syntax.

Syntax seeks to arrive at general statements about what is a sentence in a natural language. The notion "sentence in a given natural language L"

is left undefined, but this does not preclude students of natural languages from manipulating sentences. Every speaker has a keen perception of what is and what is not a sentence in his own language. If, from a given list of words (e.g., the entries of a dictionary), we proceed to build sequences, all speakers of the language will reach consistent judgments about which are sentences and which are not. For example, given the list {*a, ate, banana, boy*}, we can build sequences such as

a ate ate,

boy ate banana a a,

a ate boy banana,

ate a banana,

a boy ate a banana.

These five sequences (or strings) are taken from the set of all possible sequences that can be built with our list of words, and there is an unbounded number of such strings, since we allow repeating a word any number of times. Speakers of English will all agree that the first four sequences are not sentences while the fifth one is a sentence. Without any precise definition, it is quite possible to manipulate the notion of sentence in a reliable way. The fact that some cases are hard to judge for sentencehood does not affect this position. For example, one might hesitate over *a banana ate a boy.* Such questionable cases do not affect this fundamental fact: Among all the strings that can be built from a set of words, few will constitute sentences or quasi-sentences. This fact makes the test of intuitive recognition highly successful.

From such observations, one can derive many interesting remarks about the processes that are used to build sentences from words. For example, given two sentences S_1 and S_2, there exists a category of words (e.g., *and, if, when*) such that when they are combined with both sentences one obtains a new sentence. Their list can be established; they are called conjunctions. We will refer to them by the symbol *Conj.* Thus, the sentences

(1) *When John makes mistakes, he is unhappy,*

(2) *If John makes mistakes, he is unhappy*

can be analyzed as

   Conj S_1, S_2.

The category *Conj* corresponds here to both *when* and *if*; S_1 and S_2 are called respectively the subordinate sentence and the main sentence. Such a description is formal, since it is given in terms of shapes that can be readily observed.

In traditional grammars some notion of "time" is usually attributed to *when*, and some notion of "logical implication" to *if*. However, these two concepts are far from being easily observable in (1) and (2). The two sentences are synonymous, and if the two "activities" (*John's making mistakes* and *John's being unhappy*) are linked in some way, it is not clear how "time" and "logical implication" can be used in the same manner to describe this link in (1) and (2), rather than other notions such as "concomittance," "immediate succession," "co-occurrence of situations," "ordering with respect to time," or hundreds of others that one can apply just as well to the relation between S_1 and S_2. Notice that the synonymy depends on the particular choice of words occurring in S_1 and S_2. The sentences

When John reads this note, he will be unhappy,

If John reads this note, he will be unhappy

are not synonymous; the first implies that eventually *John* will read the note, but the second makes no such guarantee. These examples show again how inadequate traditional categories of meaning can be.

In the example above, it is not too difficult to sort out the formal from the semantic parameters of the description. In other cases it is not as obvious, even for very common terms like "subject" or "object" of a verb.

When one describes in formal terms the main parts of English sentences, one immediately observes that verbs often have to their left a noun phrase (e.g., *John, a big cake, the boy*) that can be described as a sequence of *a* (or *the*), and of categories such as "noun," "adjective," and so on. Such a sequence imposes on the verb a suffix of person-number agreement (i.e., *-s* in *John knows the boy*). To the right of a verb one can sometimes find one or more sequences of exactly the same type [i.e., the complement(s)]. Independently of such observations, when grammarians and logicians talk about sentences, they apply to them semantic notions such as action, process, state, and the like. It is considered that a sentence corresponds to an action (or a state, and so on) and that this meaning is introduced by a verb of the corresponding type. At the same time, the previously mentioned noun phrase to the left of the verb is called the subject; it performs the action. A complement noun phrase (a noun phrase occurring to the right of the verb) is called the object; it undergoes the action of the verb. This is another instance of how semantic notions are projected on formal descriptions. Although the notions "perform," "action," "undergo" are not very clear, they can, to a certain extent, be better recognized and applied by users of English than the semantic notions of the conjunction example cited previously. But in some cases the formal and the semantic terms do not coincide at all.

In the sentence

Mary chased a boy

these notions do not raise any problem: *Mary* acts, *chasing* is an action, and *a boy* undergoes some action. But in sentences such as

My report is undergoing important changes,
Making faces amuses Paul,
This hat contains twelve rabbits

the formal definitions and the semantic ones do not match at all. *To undergo* and *to contain* are not actions, and their subject and object have relations with the verb that are quite different from those that *Mary* and *boy* have with *to chase*. *Making faces* is itself an action, and it is not clear whether it "acts" in the process of *amusing*. In fact, if we consider the related sentence

John amuses Paul

we notice that it is ambiguous. We can paraphrase it by

John purposely amuses Paul

and

John is amusing to Paul.

We can describe these two meanings by qualifying the subject-verb relations in terms such as "voluntary," "volitional," or "active" on the one hand, and "nonvoluntary," "nonvolitional," or "nonactive" on the other. The relation between *making faces* and *amuses* appears to be of the "nonactive" type.

Independently of these observations, we can define a formal notion of subject by using its sequential position (i.e., left of the verb) and the presence of certain endings it imposes on the verb (e.g., *-s*). In the preceding sentences, *report*, *making faces*, *hat*, and *John* (with both interpretations) are all formal subjects.

Traditional grammar has attempted to generalize semantic notions such as subject and object to all cases of formal subjects, formal objects, and so on, but then these notions become so opaque that they are useless. Traditional grammar has also kept the two facets of description completely intermingled, while structural linguistics rejects all semantic definitions as starting points.

Linguistics then is first of all a purely combinatorial study of shapes; it consists in recognizing basic shapes and in characterizing their combinations for a given language. To characterize a language is to describe all the sentences of the language and at the same time to exclude all the nonsentences. In linguistic reasoning, as a consequence, one has to refer to nonsentences, thus making an important use of certain nongrammatical strings (such strings will be preceded by an asterisk).

By comparing the data and the findings obtained in this framework for a certain number of natural languages, linguists ought to be led to much more general statements that should apply to all languages—that should lead, in other words, to linguistic universals.[1]

1.1.2
MATHEMATICAL LOGIC

Linguistics has been influenced by different branches of mathematical logic. Traditionally, logicians have been interested in the relations between logical operators, and their counterparts in natural languages (AND, OR, IF . . . THEN, modalities, and so on), and also in deeper questions of meaning and reference (i.e., relations between names and objects of the universes they consider).

As mathematical theories became more formalized, the form they were given was the following. A set of axioms is defined, and rules of inference allow a purely formal (i.e., mechanical) derivation of theorems starting with the axioms. Theorems are considered as the sentences of a language, and the set of axioms with the rules of inference as its grammar. Formal languages used for describing such languages are called metalanguages. Logicians also provide for the interpretation of such a syntactic system: Well-defined rules associate the forms of the language with their meaning.

Both the framework and the terminology of logic evoke the description of natural languages. Various types of formal systems to be presented here were in fact devised for the description of mathematics; only later were they introduced in the study of natural languages. Z. S. Harris[2] was the first linguist to indicate this direction of research: "The work of analysis leads right up to the statements which enable anyone to synthesize or to predict utterances in the language. These statements form a deductive system with axiomatically defined initial elements, and with theorems concerning the relations among them. The final theorems would indicate the structure of the utterances of the language in terms of the preceding parts of the system."

1.1.3
COMPUTATION

Both the theory and the technology of computation involve concepts that are relevant to the study of language.

---

[1] Cf. N. Chomsky, preface to M. Gross and A. Lentin, *Introduction to Formal Grammars*, trans. M. Salkoff (Heidelberg, New York: Springer-Verlag., 1970).

[2] Z. S. Harris, *Structural Linguistics* (Chicago: The University of Chicago Press, 1951), pp. 372–73.

Theories of computation are very abstract, bearing little relation to practical calculations. Their aim is to provide a formal definition of the intuitive notion of computability. Given the usual meaning of "computable," the number π is not computable, since it has an infinite number of unpredictable decimals; but any finite approximation to it is computable.

Given a person's name and address, his phone number is computable (it can be looked up in the phone book).

Given a polynomial in the variable x, its derivative is computable.

These examples illustrate the extension of the notion of computation, and also some of its characteristics. Computation cannot be separated from the notion of "algorithm," which is the mechanical process by which a computation is performed. Algorithmic computations operate only on discrete elements, and on a finite number of them at a time (although numbers of elements can be potentially unbounded). The rules of a computation are always finite in number and in size. They are put to use by a computing agent (e.g., a human being with pencil and paper, an electronic computer) that includes a finite amount of memory (e.g., paper, magnetic devices) that can also be expanded at will.[3] Algorithms have been rigorously defined for various theoretical purposes, the main forms being Turing machines, Thue systems, Markov algorithms, formal systems, and their different variants. All turn out to be equivalent in the following sense: whatever computation can be performed with one of these devices can also be performed by any of the others. A more general statement is Church's thesis, according to which all devices that formalize the notion of computability are equivalent.

The growth in use of electronic computers had an impact on formal linguistics. In the 1950's, increased speed and memory capacity suggested that computers could serve as models for certain intellectual activities. Among these was the processing of natural language. Two new fields grew rapidly: mechanical translation and information retrieval. It was believed that with enough speed, and enough memory, it would be possible to process natural languages in a way useful for technical purposes. Soon, however, it became clear that the linguistic methods were insufficient to deal with these problems in any practical way. Mechanical translation never went much beyond the word-for-word stage, and information retrieval is now essentially limited to retrieval techniques that have little to do with linguistics. But the interest in formal methods that has grown from these two fields has certainly contributed to the rapid development of theoretical linguistics. In fact, if theoretical linguistics could reach its ultimate goal, which is an entirely explicit description of all linguistic phenomena, mechanical translation and

---

[3] This refinement of the notion of algorithm is due to Hartley Rodgers, Jr., *Theory of Recursive Functions and Effective Computability* (New York: McGraw-Hill, Inc., 1967). He adds the condition that the computations should be deterministic—that is, that each step should be entirely determined by the preceding one(s).

information retrieval as they were first defined could conceivably be domains of engineering application. But even the spectacular advances of recent years still leave linguistics far short of such a stage.

Computer techniques and mathematical linguistics are linked in still another way. For practical uses, computation algorithms are first defined in mathematical or logical form, then are implemented on computers. Computers accept algorithms only when they are written in terms of a fixed set of elementary computer instructions. Not every sequence of such instructions is meaningful. There are rules for combining them, which constitute the grammar of a language.

The language of elementary computer instructions is rather opaque. It is well adapted to the electronic organs of the machine, but it does not match the mathematical, logical, or other concepts needed for the description of algorithms. For example, a machine will have instructions such as

ADD (x, y),   MULTIPLY (x, y),

that perform additions and multiplications on two numbers x and y. These instructions are rather remote from an algorithm that would solve equations such as

$$ax^2 + bx + c = 0.$$

This equation can be solved mathematically in terms of additions and multiplications, but other instructions that have no mathematical meaning are also needed.

In a computer, additions and multiplications operate only at fixed locations of the machine. Thus, partial results have to be stored in locations where they will not interfere with the adding and multiplying mechanisms. This is obtained by means of transfer instructions such as

TRANSFER (x, a)

that will move the number x from an adder to the location a of the memory; a (a number) is called an *address*. Another type of transfer instruction will move numbers from the address where they are stored to an adder or a multiplier.

It is the role of the human programmer to write algorithms using elementary instructions. The corresponding sequences of instructions are called *programs*. To facilitate this writing procedure, other programming languages have been invented that are halfway between machine languages and the concepts needed for the descriptions of algorithms. The best known of such programming languages, sometimes called problem-oriented languages, are ALGOL and FORTRAN for mathematical problems involving numbers and COBOL for accounting problems. Algorithms are written using the instructions of these languages, and the resulting programs are automatically translated by the computer into programs written in machine language.

For example, a language for programming algorithms that computes the roots of algebraic equations would contain the operation SQUARE ROOT (x), an operation which makes it simpler for the programmer to write algorithms. The operation SQUARE ROOT (x), which does not appear in machine language, would be automatically translated into a sequence of elementary machine operations such as ADD (x, y), MULTIPLY (x, y), TRANSFER (x, a), and so on, and the programmer need not be concerned with transferring numbers to the proper locations.

Programming languages are defined by larger instructions (macro-instructions), and there are rules for combining them. These rules again constitute the grammar of the language, and they are also used in the trans-lation process into machine language.

It is interesting that certain of the methods by which the syntax of programming languages is specified originated from linguistics. Some of the formal grammars that we will study (C-languages, K-languages, and so on), were devised mainly for the description of natural languages; later they turned out to be more useful for programming languages. This field has developed considerably. Descriptions by formal methods have been studied, syntactic analyzers that use special classes of grammars have been built, and mathe-matical methods have been applied to the study of their properties.

1.2

Basic Mathematical Concepts

1.2.1
SETS

We will use the standard concepts of set theory. Capital letters repre-sent sets, lower-case letters their elements.

$A = \{a, b, c, \ldots\}$ means that the set A is composed of the elements $a, b, c, \ldots$.

$A = \{a_i : p < i \leqslant q\}$ where i, p, q are integers, means that the set A is composed of $q - p$ elements indexed by i, which can be greater than p and smaller or equal to q, they are noted as

$$a_{p+1}, a_{p+2}, \ldots, a_{q-2}, a_{q-1}, a_q.$$

$a \in A$ means that the element a belongs to the set A.

$a \notin A$ means that a does not belong to A.

$A = B$ means that the set A and the set B have the same members.

$A \subset B$ indicates that all the members of A are in B.

$A \nsubseteq B$ indicates that $A \subset B$, but also that there are elements of B that are not in A. In other words, A is properly included in B.

$\mathfrak{I}(A)$ is the set of all subsets of A.

The phrase *one of them* can be interpreted in terms of the preceding definitions: *them* corresponds to a set (a set of men, for example, as in *one of the men*), which we will denote as {*them*}. It is understood then that the element *one* belongs to (is a member of) this set, namely that

$$one \in \{them\}.$$

There is another way of representing this intuitive relation. We could consider that *one* corresponds not to an element but to a set containing only one element. Accordingly, we would write {*one*} for this set and represent the meaning of the phrase by

$$\{one\} \subset \{them\}$$

or more precisely by

$$\{one\} \not\subseteq \{them\}$$

since the two sets are such (singular and plural, respectively) that they cannot be identical. Also, the interpretation of the phrase *several of them* is unique. The symbol $\in$ cannot be used directly; we have to write

$$\{several\} \not\subseteq \{them\}.$$

In the same way, the phrase *all of them* is interpreted with

$$\{all\} = \{them\}.$$

$A = B \cup C$	A is the union of B and C; A is composed of the elements that are in B or in C, or, of course, in both B and C, and nothing else.
$A = B \cap C$	A is the intersection of B and C; A is composed of the elements that are both in B and C, and nothing else.
$A = B \setminus C$	means that the set A is the complement of C with respect to B. This identity is sometimes written $A = B - C$.
$A = B \times C$	A is the cartesian product of B and C, namely, that set containing all ordered pairs (b, c) such that $b \in B$ and $c \in C$, and nothing else; the ordered pair (b, c) is, in general, different from the ordered pair (c, b).
$\varnothing$	will be the empty set, the set that contains no members. The use of the symbol $\varnothing$ is convenient for writing certain statements compactly. For example, to express that two sets A and B do not share any element, we write $A \cap B = \varnothing$.
card $(A) = n$	means that the cardinality (i.e., the number of elements) of the set A is n. n can be infinite; we then write $card(A) = \infty$. If we apply this notation to some of the examples above, we have

$$card(\{a_i : p < i \leqslant q\}) = q - p, \qquad card(\{them\}) \geqslant 2.$$

Relations, Mappings, Operations

The elements of two given sets A and B can be related. For example, an English-French dictionary establishes a translation relation between a set A of English words and a set B of French words. It is convenient to express a relation between two sets in the form of a table. Let

$$A = \{a_1, a_2, \ldots, cavity, \ldots, hollow, \ldots, to\ know, \ldots, a_n\},$$

$$B = \{b_1, b_2, \ldots, cavité, \ldots, connaître, \ldots, savoir, \ldots, b_n\}.$$

We represent the translation relation by the accompanying table. A mark

	b_1	b_2	*cavité*	*connaître*	*savoir*	b_n
a_1						×
a_2	×					
cavity			×			
hollow			×			
to know				×	×	
a_n						×

placed at the crossing of a line and a column indicates that the word written on the column is a translation of the word written in the line. If we name the relation Tr, we can also write

$$a_1\ Tr\ b_n, \ldots, hollow\ Tr\ cavité, \ldots, a_n\ Tr\ b_n,$$

to describe the relation.

A varied terminology and different corresponding notations are available, depending on the use and shape of the relation.

Each pair made of the headings of one line and one column represents an element of the cartesian product $A \times B$. A relation can thus be looked at as a subset of $A \times B$, the subset that corresponds to the marked pairs.

We can also say that the table represents a "mapping" from A to B. Calling this mapping Tr, we write equivalently

$$Tr(a_1) = b_n, \ldots, Tr(hollow) = cavité, \ldots, Tr(a_n) = b_n,$$

and we say, for example, that b_n is the image of a_1.

More generally, let f be a mapping between A and B. f can be "many-to-one." It may then associate several elements of A to one element $b_j \in B$. In terms of the table of f, the marks in the column of b_j determine the elements of A that are mapped (i.e., associated) to b_j. Our dictionary Tr can be many-to-one, since for $b_j = cavité$, we have

$$Tr(cavity) = Tr(hollow) = cavité.$$

When f is many-to-one, it is convenient to use the inverse mapping of f; we write f^{-1} for this inverse mapping. When we write $f^{-1}(b_j)$, $b_j \in B$, then $f^{-1}(b_j) \subset A$; $f^{-1}(b_j)$ is the subset C of A whose elements all have b_j for their image (i.e., $f(C) = b_j$). In our example,

$$Tr^{-1}(cavité) = \{cavity, hollow\}.$$

Mappings can be "one-to-many," Tr that associates two different French verbs to the verb *to know* has this property:

$$Tr(to\ know) = \{connaître, savoir\}.$$

A mapping is "one-to-one" when it associates one single element of A to one single element of B. The distribution of marks in the corresponding table is such that each line and each column contains at most one mark.

The same types of correspondences can be stated within the single set A, namely between A and A. We can also define operations in the set A. A binary operation defined on a set A is a "two-to-one" mapping, or a relation between the cartesian product $A \times A$ and A. A binary operation associates a pair of elements a and b of A [i.e., $(a, b) \in A \times A$] to $c \in A$. There are various notations for operations. We can write

$$(a, b) \longrightarrow c$$

or, in the form of a product,

$$ab = c$$

or, as a sum,

$$a + b = c$$

or we can use a special symbol for the operation, such as

$$a \otimes b = c.$$

An operation can be unary, applying to a single element (e.g., the inversion that associates to a number n the number $1/n$), or it can be k-ary; it is then defined as a subset of the cartesian product

$$\underbrace{A \times A \times \cdots \times A.}_{k+1\,A\text{'s}}$$

In general an operation on A does not have to be defined on all elements (e.g., on all pairs of $A \times A$ for a binary operation). But in practice operations are quite regular—that is, defined everywhere. The same is true for mappings (f) between A and B. For example, we will be able to write $f(A) = B$ if each element of A has an image in B, and if each element of B has some "inverse" image in A.

Morphisms

We will now combine the two notions of operations and mapping. We will consider two sets A and B. For each set some operation is defined everywhere. Also a mapping φ is defined between A and B ($\varphi(A) = B$).

In general, the two operations defined on A and B are unrelated, but sometimes some similarity can be observed between them. Certain types of similarities can be expressed by φ.

In the general case, the operations in A and B are unrelated (Figure 1.1). The correspondence φ associates to a_1, a_2 ($\in A$), the elements b_1, b_2 ($\in B$), respectively. φ is many-to-one: $\varphi(a_2) = \varphi(a_4) = b_2$. On the other hand, the definition of the operation in A (noted as a product) gives $a_1a_2 = a_3$; similarly

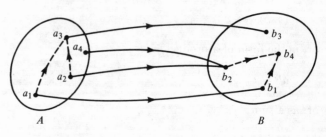

A B

FIGURE 1.1

in B we have $b_1b_2 = b_4$. The associations made by the operations are indicated in the figures by dotted lines with arrows. Since the operations in A and B are not related, the element $\varphi(a_3) = b_3$ (image of the product a_1a_2) has nothing to do with b_4 (the product b_1b_2).

In Figure 1.2 the operations in A and B are related (i.e., similar in some sense). The situation differs from that in Figure 1.1 only in that b_3 and b_4 have

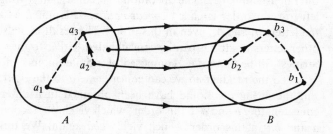

FIGURE 1.2

merged, and this will be the case for all products of two elements that correspond by φ. We will have

$$\varphi(a_1a_2) = \varphi(a_1)\varphi(a_2), \qquad \text{for all } a_1, a_2 \in A$$

φ is still many-to-one. It is called a morphism, and $\varphi(A) = B$ is the morphic image of A.

In Figure 1.3 the situation is different. φ is still a morphism, but φ is also one-to-one. It is called an isomorphism. Isomorphisms express very strong resemblances between sets with operations. The sets must have the same number of elements, and the operations have to correspond very closely.

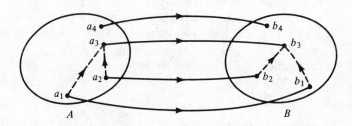

FIGURE 1.3

1.2.2
STRINGS

We will often use sets that we call *alphabets* (their elements are called *letters*) or *vocabularies* (their elements are then called *words*). From the formal point of view, there is no difference other than terminological.

We will use these elements (letters or words) to build *strings*—sequences oriented from left to right, as we do in ordinary writing with the letters of the English alphabet. The operation that consists in writing two letters in the left-to-right order is called *concatenation*. It is noted as a product: *ab* for the letters *a*, and *b*, given in this order. The result is the string *ab*, to which other letters or strings can be concatenated, either to the right or to the left. Strings will be finite (i.e., composed of a finite number of letters).

To the product *ab* we can concatenate *a* to the right, the result is *aba*. But the string *aba* could have been obtained in a different way: first by concatenating *b* and *a* in this order, which yields *ba*, second by concatenating *a* and *ba* in this order, which yields *aba* again. We thus have $[(ab)a] = [a(ba)] = aba$. The parentheses indicate the ways concatenation has been applied. More generally, when a product of three elements is such that the order in which the elements are multiplied does not change the final result, it is called *associative*.

Some operations are not associative. Consider, for example, the three words *brown*, *bird's*, and *nest*. There are two ways of associating them in this order:

[brown (bird's nest)],   [(brown bird's) nest].

The two meanings of the sequence *brown bird's nest* correspond in a natural manner to the two ways of combining the individual words. The syntactic operation that combines these words is not associative.

With sets of strings, special operations and notations are quite natural.

If *A* is a set of letters (i.e., an alphabet), A^* is the set of all strings that can be built by means of the letters of *A*. *A* is, in general, finite, and each string is finite, but A^* is infinite, since the number of occurrences of letters that compose a string has no upper limit.

It is convenient to talk about the null or empty string, a string made of zero letters, which we shall write as *e*. Since it is a string, and not a letter, *e* does not belong to *A*. The null string *e* is a unit element with respect to concatenation; if *f* is a string, we have

$$fe = ef = f.$$

Concatenating the null string to the left or the right of a string *f* does not change *f*. By definition, A^* contains *e*. The null string *e* plays exactly the role of the number 1 in multiplications: $1 \times n = n \times 1 = n$, and of the number 0 in additions: $0 + n = n + 0 = n$, where n is a number (i.e., 1 and 0 are the neutral elements of multiplication and addition, respectively).

EXAMPLE _____

The alphabet A consists of one letter a: $A = \{a\}$. We then have

$$A^* = \{e, a, aa, aaa, \ldots, aaaa \ldots a, \ldots\}.$$

A^* is composed, in addition to e, of all sequences of a's. Notice that when we write a by itself, there is a new ambiguity, a can be a letter (we write $a \in A$), or it can be a string of one letter (we will then write $a \in A^*$).

We wrote $A \times B$ for the cartesian product of the two sets A and B. When A and B are sets of strings, the notation indicating the product (i.e., the concatenation) of the two sets will be AB. AB will be the set of all strings that can be obtained by taking any string f of A and by concatenating to its right any string g of B. For all $f \in A$, and for all $g \in B$, we have $fg \in AB$.

When $A = B$, the product AA will be written A^2; A^3 is the product of A^2 by A (or of A by A^2), and so on. This notation is justified by the fact that concatenation is associative (for example, $(AA)A = A(AA) = A^3$).

We use the same notation for strings. A sequence of n successive a's is written a^n:

$$aaa = a^3, \qquad aaaabb = a^4b^2.$$

This power notation is more than a notation. It allows calculus in the same way as with variables in classical algebra. If we concatenate aaa (i.e., a^3) and $aaaabb$ (i.e., a^4b^2), we obtain $aaaaaaabb$, which we write as a^7b^2. In other words, the powers add together. We also have $a^0 = e$. The powers give a measure of the length of a string counted in number of letters. For the length of a string f we will use the notations $|f|$ (length of f), or else $d^0(f)$ (degree of f). We have thus

$$|aaaabb| = d^0(aaaabb) = 6.$$

We will also write $d_a^0(f)$ for degree in a of the word f (i.e., number of occurrences of a in f).

In § 1.3.4 we give examples of the use of these notations in phonology.

*1.2.3
MONOIDS

A monoid is a set M, finite or infinite with an operation associating one element of M to every pair of elements of M. The operation is associative. Noting it as a product, we have

for all $x, y, z \in M$, $\qquad x(yz) = (xy)z$.

A monoid always contains an identity element e, so that

for all $x \in M$, $ex = xe = x$.

A monoid without its identity element is called a semigroup.

The operation need not be commutative; that is, we can have

for some (or all) $x, y \in M$, $xy \neq yx$.

This is the case for concatenation.

The basic set M is sometimes called the set of the generators of the monoid when all the elements of the monoid can be built from the elements of M. (We should then have two names—one, M, for the set itself, and another for M together with its operation.)

An example of a monoid is the set of integers $\{i: i > 0\}$ together with the operation of ordinary multiplication.

Given a set X of generators, and a product operation, we say that X generates a free monoid X^*, if X^* is a monoid, and its elements can be factorized (i.e., decomposed) in a unique manner[4] in terms of products of the elements of X.

As another example justifying the star (i.e., asterisk) in the paragraph above, let us take an alphabet X and the operation of concatenation, which is associative and noncommutative. The identity element is the null string e; the other elements of X^* are the strings that can be formed by means of the letters of X. The elements of X^* have a unique factorization property in terms of the letters of X: Spelling out from left to right the letters that compose a string provides us with its factorization. X^* is then the same object as the one defined above.

Another example of a free monoid X^* is $X = \{aa, ab\}$, and the operation is still concatenation. The generators do not consist any longer in single letters. Any string composed by concatenating aa's and ab's is uniquely factorizable by scanning the string from one end, looking at two letters at a time.

1.2.4
POLYNOMIALS AND SERIES
ON STRINGS

By means of the product (concatenation) of sets, and by union, we can construct expressions such as

$(AB \cup C)$, $(D \cup A)$,

---

[4] It does not follow from the definition that a free monoid exists. One has to give a proof and preferably a way to construct at least one. Cf. C. Chevalley, *Fundamental Concepts of Algebra* (New York: Academic Press, Inc., 1956).

that correspond to sets of strings. We will generalize this notation, replacing the union by a new commutative operation on sets denoted by $+$. Consider the expression $A + B$. When A and B are disjoint (i.e., $A \cap B = \varnothing$), we have $A + B = A \cup B$; the two operations are not distinguished. When A and B have common elements ($A \cap B = C \neq \varnothing$), within the union set ($A \cup B$) the elements of C lose all distinction as to their origin; it is meaningless to say that they originate from A rather than from B; but in the sum $A + B$ the common elements are counted twice, which is indicated by the positive integer 2. More generally, in expressions more complex than the union of two sets—for example, in expressions involving concatenation of sets—identical elements may be added more than twice. Then a positive integer is adjoined to each element in order to count the number of occurrences of that element in the sets of these expressions.

More technically, given a set X (an alphabet), the set of polynomials that we define informally here is called a free semi-ring.

EXAMPLE I _____

A set $A = \{a_i: 0 \leqslant i \leqslant n\}$ can be represented as the (commutative) sum of its elements

$$A = a_0 + a_1 + a_2 + \cdots + a_i + \cdots + a_n.$$

In fact, we ought to write

$$A = 1a_0 + 1a_1 + \cdots + 1a_n,$$

since in a set each element appears only once.

EXAMPLE II _____

The product AB of the two expressions

$$A = (a + ab) \quad \text{and} \quad B = (e + b + a)$$

is written

$$(a + ab)(e + b + a),$$

and is obtained, as in ordinary algebra, by multiplying all elements of A by all elements of B; the only difference is that the product is noncommutative. We multiply by a, on the left, all members of the second factor (i.e., B), obtaining

$$a + ab + aa.$$

Then we multiply the members of B by ab, which gives

$$ab + abb + aba.$$

Adding, we obtain

$$AB = a + 2ab + aa + abb + aba$$
$$= a + 2ab + a^2 + ab^2 + aba.$$

[*Note:* The expression B is different from $B = b + a$. Here the use of e makes an important difference.]

EXAMPLE III

We transform the expression

$$A = (b + bab)a(b + bab).$$

Multiplying, we obtain

$$A = bab + 2babab + bababab.$$

Factoring out *bab* to the left,

$$A = bab(e + 2ab + abab).$$

Further, factoring out *ab* to the right inside the parentheses,

$$A = bab[e + (2 + ab)ab].$$

EXAMPLE IV

We multiply $A = e + 2ab$ by $B = e + 3ab$, obtaining

$$AB = e + 5ab + 6abab.$$

The coefficient 6 corresponds to our interpretation: There are $2ab$'s in A, and 3 in B, thus there are 6 ways to combine them to obtain *abab*.

When they are composed of a finite number of term, such expressions are called *polynomials in noncommutative variables*. When they have an infinite number of terms, they are called *power series*.

EXAMPLE V

Consider the expression

$$(the + this + a)\, girl\, (came + arrived)\, (early + late).$$

It is a polynomial in English words. When the product is developed, the result is the sum of 12 English sentences. We will use this notation when we will have to state in a compact way large numbers of structurally related examples. Usually, for the same types of examples, linguists use braces instead of parentheses:

$$\begin{Bmatrix} the \\ this \\ a \end{Bmatrix} girl \begin{Bmatrix} came \\ arrived \end{Bmatrix} \begin{Bmatrix} early \\ late \end{Bmatrix}.$$

1.3

Applications to Natural Languages

We now present some elementary uses of the notions we just have described.

1.3.1
BASIC PROPERTIES OF LANGUAGES

The mathematical definitions we have just given concern discrete elements only. We will be dealing, for example, with abstract algebra, combinatorial analysis, and so on, but not with real numbers or differential equations. This restriction in the use of mathematics is due to empirical observations about natural languages.

Language is discrete—a remark that should not be taken as obvious. For a physical receiver (any acoustic or electronic device) the sound that comes out of the vocal tract of a human being is continuous. The acoustic parameters that can be attached to the flow of speech (intensity, pitch, and so on) are continuous with respect to time. From the psychological point of view, however, it is clear that speech is discrete in some sense; it is composed of discontinuous elements. Moreover, these elements (elementary sounds or phonemes) recur constantly. One of the best proofs for the discrete nature of language is that alphabetic writing is possible. Alphabetic writing, in fact, indicates two types of segmentation into discrete units. On the one hand, sentences can be considered as sequences of letters (or phonemes); on the other, they can be analyzed as sequences of words.

A given alphabet V determines a set V^*. By definition, a formal language L on the alphabet V is a subset of V^*:

$$L \subset V^*.$$

Given an alphabet of phonemes V, not every string on V constitutes a word in the language. For example, a string of five consonants such as *brtsm* is not a conceivable part of a word in English. The set of the words W of a language is thus properly included in V^*, which is the set of all possible strings of phonemes. We write then

$$W \nsubseteq V^*.$$

Notice that the set L of all possible sentences of a language is also a proper subset of V^*, but it is much more meaningful to define sentences in terms of words (or morphemes) rather than directly in terms of phonemes. Of course, not all sequences of words are sentences. We then have the relations

$$L \nsubseteq W^* \nsubseteq V^*.$$

Units such as phonemes or words (or morphemes) are always found in finite numbers. In fact, linguists and lexicographers have established exhaustive lists of them. The set V of the phonemes of a natural language is usually composed of from 10 to 60 phonemes. The set W of words in a natural language also is finite, but may number several hundreds of thousands. There is no explanation for the fact that W is finite. Words or morphemes could a priori be of unbounded length. However, it turns out that for many languages some upper bound on the length can always be observed. We can state safely that for English, there are no words of length greater than 50 phonemes, although we cannot explain why.

For sentences (or discourses), which are conveniently described in terms of words, it is impossible to establish exhaustive lists. The reason is simple. The length of a sentence may grow indefinitely. We can give no empirical upper bound as we did for words. We could venture that no sentence in English has a length greater than say, 10,000 (counted in number of morphemes), a proposition that could be verified by a straightforward study of texts. However, the situation is quite different from that for words—for at least two reasons.

First, to utter sentences in terms of words is an extraordinarily productive and varied process. In fact, actual sentences are rarely repeated. If we were to look in all the texts of a large library (not containing this book!), trying to find in them the sentence

Mary is, to me, a very beautiful woman

as it is written here, word for word, chances are that we would never observe it, although it looks common and simple. This productivity is easily observed in sets of sentences like the following:

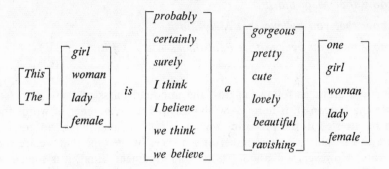

A sentence is constructed choosing one word from each set. We have $2 \times 4 \times 7 \times 6 \times 5 = 1{,}680$ sentences, and it is clear that they all have close meanings. By using only synonyms or quasi-synonyms, it is easy to build in this way sets of sentences of length 20 that have a cardinality of the order of 10^{50}, which also suggests that it will be hard to perform on texts any statistical study involving actual sentences.

Second, some syntactic processes, such as conjunction, have the property of being recurrent (or recursive); they involve operations that can reapply any number of times. Consider the sentence

John is strong, and stupid.

We can insert an adjective into it, say *tall* to right of *is*:

John is tall, strong, and stupid.

We can repeat the insertion on the resulting sentence:

John is fat, tall, strong, and stupid

into which we can again insert an adjective, yielding

John is dirty, fat, tall, strong, and stupid.

This insertion process can go on indefinitely. There is no upper bound on the length of sentences that can be produced in this way.

Similarly, certain constructions such as *I know that . . . , you believe that . . . , Paul thinks that . . .* , may be combined in an unbounded way:

I know that Mary did it

I know that you believe that Mary did it

I know that you believe that Paul thinks Mary did it.

. . . .

We could argue as follows against the unboundedness of these processes. Since the lexicon W is finite, it would seem that the number of words that can be inserted in the preceding sentences is also finite, which means that there can be only a finite number of sentences of the type that we are considering. However, we cannot use such an argument. First, it is sometimes possible to repeat certain verbs any number of times:

I know that you know that Paul knows . . . that Mary did it.

Moreover, the number of verbs in a language is a property of the culture. There might be large differences across languages, according to the presence of technical terms. It seems quite unreasonable to link this cultural fact to the recursive process of subordination. Grammatical and lexical studies have always been kept apart. Using the size of the lexicon to describe a grammatical process would only blur a separation that has thus far proved extremely useful.

Other processes also can generate sentences of unbounded length—relative-clause adjunctions, for example—and the same arguments can be repeated for them. Many observations of this type have forced linguists to consider natural languages as infinite sets of strings.

We can now summarize our results about the relation

$$L \nsubseteq W^* \nsubseteq V^*.$$

We have

$$card\ (L) = \infty, \qquad card\ (W) \approx 10^5, \qquad card\ (V) \simeq 35.$$

It is difficult to give more than orders of magnitude, since precise numbers depend very much on the language and on how the elements are counted.

1.3.2
FACTORIZATION OF STRINGS

We mentioned factorization in defining the free monoid. To factorize a string in terms of a basic set of letters or of strings is to analyze it in terms of these items—that is, to indicate how they are combined to form the string. Although sentences are, first of all, sequences of phonemes, they are best analyzed in terms of words. Traditional grammar performs such analysis in the following way.

Sentences are analyzed in terms of grammatical categories. The sentence

(S)   John is an amusing fellow

can be analyzed from left to right as: N_{pr} (proper name), V (verb), At (article), Adj (adjective), N (noun). These symbols are in a set G distinct from V (or V^*), and there are relations between G^* and W^* (the set of strings on words). But factorization (i.e., analysis) is a quite complex process for natural languages. Alternatively, the sentence (S) can be quite meaningfully factorized as: NP (noun phrase), V (verb), NP (noun phrase). We now have two different factorizations for (S), both of which are syntactically significant. Moreover, a factorization like NP, VP (verb phrase) can also be used for (S). The relations between these various analyses are by no means obvious, considering that they are related by mappings of a morphic type.

The situation is even more complex for sentences such as

(T)   They are flying planes

which have two interpretations—one corresponding to one of the analyses that we gave for (S): N, V, Adj, N, and the other to the analysis N, V, N. We have

They N	are V	flying Adj	planes N

and

They N	are flying V	planes N

We can also indicate the two factorizations by means of parentheses:

(They are (flying planes)),
(They (are flying) planes).

We will see that the problem of analyzing sentences is in fact the central problem in linguistics, and most of the formal devices that we will describe in this book have been devised to deal with these questions.

1.3.3
POLYNOMIALS ON PHONEMES

Let us consider the list of all initial consonant clusters in English words. This list can be obtained by looking up the initial consonantal segments in an English dictionary. For clusters of length greater than one, leaving out the glides *w* and *y*, we find[5]

spr, str, skr, spl, skl,

sf, sm, sn, sl, sp, sk, st,

pr tr, kr, br, dr, fr, gr, sr, θr, pl, kl, fl, bl, gl.

We can write this list as a polynomial in the noncommutative variables *C* (consonants). We need only replace the commas by $+$ signs. It turns out that the list can be rewritten in the following form:

$$(P) \quad [(e + s)(p + k) + b + f + g](l + r)$$
$$+ [(e + s)t + \check{s} + d + \theta]r + s(f + m + n + p + k + l + t)$$

where *e* is the null string.

What we have just done reminds one of high school algebra homework, where a polynomial in several commutative variables is to be factored into a product of sums. Such polynomials are especially built for the purpose. The textbook writer starts from a product of factors, does all the multiplications, and asks for the inverse process. If one tries to transform into a product of factors a polynomial whose terms are randomly chosen, the chances are small that a result can be obtained. Only very special polynomials have this factoring property. What we did above, however, was to start with a list found in a dictionary; there was no reason to suspect it would not be random. We succeeded in writing the list as a product of factors, which by itself demonstrates that the list is very remarkable, and asks for an explanation. In this instance a simple formal technique applied to a list of observations has led to the discovery of a certain structure, evidence of some internal organization.

We attempted to factor the list of initial consonant clusters on purely formal grounds, trying to get as many products as we could. We also singled out the variable *s*, and we obtained a polynomial where *s* has a remarkable position. The result is a formula revealing that the factors are phonologically significant, which ought to come as a surprise.

---

[5] The sound θ corresponds to the letter *th* in *thing*; the sound *k* corresponds to the letters *k* and *c* as in *akin* and *acorn*; *š* is *sh* in *shrill*. These data are part of Harris' description (*Structural Linguistics*, p. 153).

We could imagine other interesting situations in this connection. Suppose that, starting with a list of elements of the size we just dealt with, we do not succeed in factoring it, only because one element is absent from the list (i.e., not observed in the data). Such a situation indicates a "gap" in the distribution. The discovery of gaps is important, since often they suggest or confirm the use of a grammar rule. The formal device of polynomials could in certain complex cases help to discover gaps where simple examination of the data might be insufficient.

1.3.4
A NOTATION IN PHONOLOGY

In phonology, certain sounds (phonemes) change in well-defined contexts. For example, the *c* of *electric* is pronounced as *s* in *electricity*. Usually contexts are defined in terms of individual phonemes or of categories of phonemes—for example, a string of consonants. Generative phonology[6] uses contexts such as "a string of any number of consonants, possibly none"; this context is noted as C_0. In the algebraic framework we defined, for this same notion we use C^*. In the same way there are contexts such as "one or more consonants" denoted as C_1, "two or more consonants" denoted as C_2. C_1 and C_2 correspond to our CC^* and C^2C^*, respectively.

It is sometimes useful to refer to the set of strings on an alphabet A that contain the given sequence $\alpha \in A^*$. The corresponding notation will be $A^*\alpha A^*$. In the same way, in order to mention the set of strings on A that do not contain the substring α, we can use the expression $A^* \setminus A^*\alpha A^*$ (complement of the set of strings that contain α). Again, if A is a set of strings, $A^k A^*$ is the set of all possible strings composed of elements of A that have at least k terms.

Our aim is now to study more complicated mathematical devices that lend themselves to the description of natural languages. After defining and studying several such systems, we shall return to their motivation in terms of empirical data.

---

[6] Cf. N. Chomsky and M. Halle, *The Sound Pattern of English* (New York: Harper & Row, Publishers, 1968), and S. Schane, *Phonology* (Englewood Cliffs, N.J.: Prentice-Hall, Inc., to appear).

Turing Machines

Turing machines[1] are abstract mechanisms,
whose purpose is to provide a formal
—thus, precise—definition of the intuitive notions
of *computation* and of *algorithm*.

2.1

Definitions

2.1.1
THE MACHINE

A Turing machine is a very simplified computer composed of a central unit and of an input-output device acting on a tape (Figure 2.1). The central unit may assume different states. Changes of state correspond roughly to changes in the memory content of the machine. The number of states is

---

[1] From the name of the British mathematician Turing who devised them.

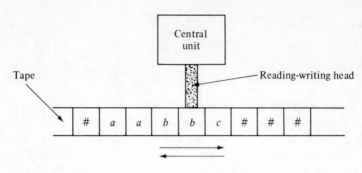

FIGURE 2.1

finite. We call Σ the set of the states of a given Turing machine:

$$\Sigma = \{S_i : 0 \leqslant i \leqslant n\}$$

where the S_i's are the different states.

The tape is divided into squares, on each of which one symbol is written. Blank squares (i.e., spaces) are indicated by the special symbol $\#$. Automata deal only with finite pieces of tape (counted in number of squares), but an indefinite supply of tape is available, if needed, during a computation.

The symbols written on the tape are finite in number. The set A of these symbols is called the alphabet of the machine

$$A = \{a_j : 0 \leqslant j \leqslant p\},$$

where a_0 will be the blank symbol $\#$.[2] Input strings will not, in general, contain the blank symbol.

The central unit and the tape are connected by means of a head that reads and writes symbols on the tape (one at a time), and that may move the tape one square to the right or one square to the left.

2.1.2
COMPUTATIONS

The steps in the computations of an automaton are defined by means of instructions that may modify the states and either the content of the square under the head or the position of the tape.

---

[2] We also use lower-case letters $a, b, c, \ldots$ for $a_1, a_2, a_3, \ldots$, respectively.

Instructions are of three types[3]

(i) $(a_i, S_j) \rightarrow (a_k, S_l)$
(ii) $(a_i, S_j) \rightarrow (R, S_l)$
(iii) $(a_i, S_j) \rightarrow (L, S_l)$.

To the left of the arrows appears the machine's situation in terms of its state and the symbol appearing under the head. To the right of the arrows are given the changes that are allowed at each step of a computation. In the three cases the situation corresponds to state S_j, and to the symbol a_i under the head. Also, in each case the central unit switches to state S_l, but the tape is modified in three different ways:

1. In case (i) the symbol a_i is replaced by the symbol a_k, and the tape is not moved.
2. In case (ii) the tape is moved one square to the right (R), and the head does not write any symbol.
3. In case (iii) the tape is moved one square to the left (L), and the head does not write any symbol.

A computation is a series of individual steps such as (i), (ii), (iii) that are chained together: when an instruction has been applied, the machine is in a new (possibly the same) situation, another instruction (possibly the same) may then be applied, and the process may continue in this way. One of two events may occur, depending both on the input and on the instructions. Either a situation is reached that does not correspond to any left member of the instructions of the machine—we then say that the automaton blocks—and the computation comes to an end, or else a sequence of instructions may reapply indefinitely, in which case the computation never ends.

Computations are usually defined in a more regular way. A special state, S_0, is distinguished as the initial state. Computations start with the machine in state S_0, with a nonnull input string on the tape, and with the head on the leftmost symbol of the input string. When the input string is null the computation may start anywhere on the blank tape. When the machine blocks, the string that appears on the tape (between blanks) is called the result of the computation, or the output.[4] If we consider the set of instructions of a Turing machine as an algorithm, all the requirements about

---

[3] S_l may be identical to S_j, and a_k to a_i.

[4] Sometimes the following requirement is imposed on the termination. A subset Σ_f of Σ is distinguished; the states of Σ_f are the final states. In order to terminate, computations have to block in one of the states of Σ_f. Computations that block in states that do not belong to Σ_f do not provide any result. We will not use this convention for Turing machines, but we will see types of automata where a similar definition is used.

discreteness and finiteness that we have mentioned (§ 1.1.3) are met by the definitions.

EXAMPLE I

The alphabet is $A = \{\#, a, b\}$, the set of states $\Sigma = \{S_0, S_1\}$, S_0 is the initial state, the instructions are

(1) $(b, S_0) \rightarrow (L, S_0)$
(2) $(a, S_0) \rightarrow (\#, S_1)$
(3) $(\#, S_1) \rightarrow (L, S_0)$.[5]

The input tape will be *baaab*.

The computation will proceed as indicated in Figure 2.2 by the movements of the tape and the changes of states of the central unit. The effect of this computation is to replace the *a*'s by blanks $\#$. In a sequence of *a*'s this is done in two steps: Instruction (2) replaces *a* by $\#$, and instruction (3) moves the tape one square to the left in order to bring a new *a* under the head. Instruction (1) allows the head to skip the *b*'s. The computation blocks, since the situation $(\#, S_0)$ is not a left member of any instruction, and the result is the string *b###b*.

Notice that we could have used the instructions

(2′) $(a, S_0) \rightarrow (\#, S_0)$
(3′) $(\#, S_0) \rightarrow (L, S_0)$

instead of (2) and (3), in order to replace the *a*'s. This would have saved one state, but then, when the head had reached the first $\#$ to the right of the second *b*, instruction (3′) would have applied indefinitely, since we have agreed that any indefinite amount of blank tape needed for the application of instructions has to be supplied to the machine. The computation would not have provided any result.

2.1.3
DETERMINICITY

We can impose the following restriction on the set of rules that define a Turing machine. We require that no more than one instruction ever applies in a given situation—that is, that the set of rules does not contain two instructions with the same left member and different right members. In this case, the machines will be called deterministic; otherwise, they will be non-deterministic.

A Turing machine can be considered as a mapping between tapes. Example I maps each tape of the form $b^m a^n b^p$ to the tape $b^m \#^n b^p$. The

---

[5] We have not quite given a characteristic function. We should have provided instructions that erase completely the input string, and then provide exactly 0 or 1 as the result of the checking procedure.

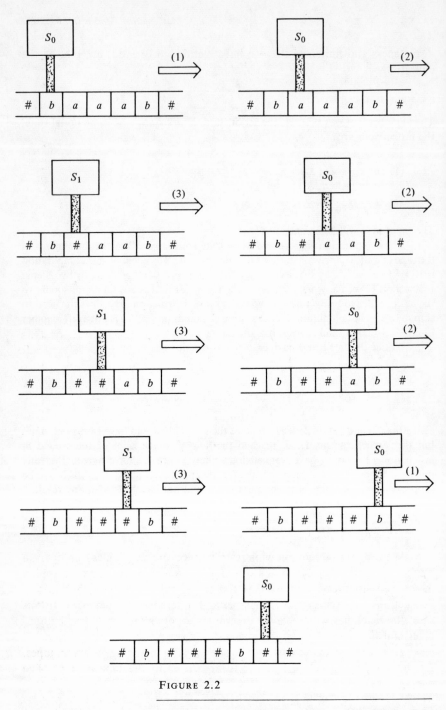

FIGURE 2.2

The computation follows the arrows; the numbers above each arrow correspond to the instructions that apply.

machine is deterministic, and the mapping is one-to-one. Nondeterministic machines correspond to one-to-many mappings. It is also possible to define many-to-one and many-to-many mappings.

EXAMPLE II

We consider the following extension of Example I:

$$A = \{\#, a, b\}, \quad \Sigma = \{S_0, S_1\}, \qquad (S_0 \text{ initial state}).$$

The instructions are

(1) $(b, S_0) \to (L, S_0)$
(2) $(a, S_0) \to (\#, S_1)$
(3) $(\#, S_1) \to (L, S_0)$

as before, and we add

(4) $(a, S_0) \to (b, S_0)$.

Instructions (2) and (4) make the machine nondeterministic. In any situation (a, S_0), one of two steps of computation is possible. The first one, as in Example I, replaces a by $\#$, whereas the other one replaces a by b. For example, after the first step of Figure 2.2, the two branches in Figure 2.3 correspond to the two possible

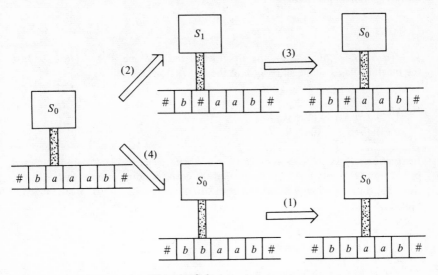

FIGURE 2.3

The two branches correspond to the two possible substitutions. After they have applied, the machine is back in the situation (a, S_0) where the computation may branch again in the same way. The machine maps the string *baaab* to 8 different strings (instead of each a we can find either $\#$ or b).

substitutions. After they have been applied, the machine is back in the situation (a, S_0), where the computation may branch again in the same way. The machine maps the string *baaab* to eight different strings (instead of each *a* we can find either # or *b*).

2.2

Definition of Languages

Turing machines can be used in various ways for defining languages. We will mention the more typical processes.

2.2.1
CHARACTERISTIC FUNCTIONS

Let V be an alphabet, V^* the set of input strings; $L \subset V^*$ is a language. A Turing machine that associates the symbol 1 to all $f \in L$, and the symbol 0 to all $g \notin L$ constitutes a characteristic function of the set L. It fulfills our requirement for a device to be a grammar of a language—that is, to be an entirely explicit mechanism.

EXAMPLE III

$V = \{a, b\}$, $L = \{a^n : n \geqslant 0\}$, the alphabet of the machine is $A = \{\#, a, b, 0, 1\}$, the machine has a single state S_0, and the instructions are

(1) $(a, S_0) \rightarrow (L, S_0)$
(2) $(\#, S_0) \rightarrow (1, S_0)$
(3) $(b, S_0) \rightarrow (0, S_0)$.

Instruction (1) skips any number of *a*'s; then, when a blank is encountered, instruction (2) prints 1, which means that the corresponding input is in L. Instruction (3) prints a 0 when *b* is met. In both situations $(1, S_0)$ and $(0, S_0)$ the machine blocks.

2.2.2
WEAK ACCEPTANCE

The preceding type of device characterizes the strings of a language $L \subset V^*$, as well as the strings of the complement of L: $V^* \setminus L$. Using the fact that in certain cases the machine computes indefinitely, we could weaken the notion of acceptance as follows. When $f \in L$, the machine prints out the symbol 1, but when $f \notin L$, the machine either blocks or goes on computing indefinitely. The process is weaker in the following way: When a computation is being performed on a string, we have no way of predicting beforehand, or at any step of the computation, whether it will ever stop or not—that is, whether the input string does or does not belong to the language. The preceding process was defined in such a way that the machine had to stop in either case. From a "practical" point of view, when one has to describe a language, the first procedure is much more satisfactory.

2.2.3
FUNDAMENTAL PROPERTIES
OF LANGUAGES

The processes we have just defined are very special, and it is by no means obvious that, given an arbitrary language $L \subset V^*$, it is always possible to construct for it one of the Turing machines of the types mentioned. In fact, quite the reverse is true.

(1) *Some languages cannot be described at all by Turing machines, whatever the process used.*

V^* is an infinite set, and it is denumerable—that is, all its elements can be ordered, say alphabetically. The set of all subsets of V^* (i.e., the set of all languages on V) is thus infinite, but not denumerable; it has the power of the continuum.

It is possible to define the set of all Turing machines. Consider an alphabet $A = \{a_j : 0 \leqslant j \leqslant p\}$, a set of states $\Sigma = \{S_i : 0 \leqslant i \leqslant n\}$, which will be used for all Turing machines. Any Turing machine (T) can be described by a string on the alphabet $B = \{\rightarrow\} \cup M \cup \Sigma$, where

$$M = \{L, R\} \cup A, m_k \in M:$$

$$s(T) = a_{j_1} S_{k_1} \rightarrow m_1 S_{l_1} a_{j_2} S_{k_2} \rightarrow m_2 S_{l_2} \cdots a_{j_q} S_{k_q} \rightarrow m_q S_{l_q}$$

This notation amounts to writing the instructions horizontally instead of vertically as in the previous examples.[6] We have the relation $s(T) \in B^*$. The set of all Turing machines is then a subset of B^*. It is infinite and denumerable, since it is possible to order alphabetically all the expressions $s(T)$.

Thus, a nondenumerable set of languages cannot be described at all by Turing machines.

---

[6] Notice that several words may correspond to a single Turing machine. The notation that we are using imposes a left-to-right ordering of the rules. A different ordering modifies the word but not the machine. Also, we can make more precise the set of all Turing machines; instead of just saying it is a subset of B^*, we can restrict it to a subset of $\{A\Sigma \rightarrow \{A, L, R\}\Sigma\}^*$ (i.e., the set of all products or strings of instructions).

(2) *The two processes (characteristic function and weak acceptance) are not equivalent.*

The languages that have a characteristic function are called the *recursive* languages; those defined by the weaker process are called the *recursively enumerable* languages. It can be proved (see, for example, M. Davis) that the class of recursive languages is properly included in the class of recursively enumerable languages—that is, that some languages cannot be defined at all by the characteristic process.

2.2.4
REMARKS

(1) Representing the classes of languages by circles, we have the relations shown in Figure 2.4.

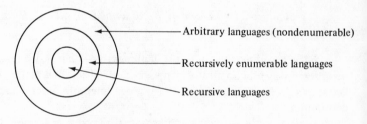

Figure 2.4

(2) For a characteristic function, the two symbols 0 and 1 play a symmetrical role. The machine defines both L and $V^* \setminus L$ (the complement of L with respect to V^*). A characteristic function is thus equivalent to the two processes of the weaker type functioning in parallel. One maps the words of L to the symbol 1, the other the words of $V^* \setminus L$ to the symbol 0. In other words, if a language and its complement are both recursively enumerable, then the language is recursive.

2.3

Extensions of Turing Machines

2.3.1
UNIVERSAL TURING MACHINES

When one talks about Turing machines performing computations, several analogies with electronic computers come to mind.

If, for example, we look at a Turing machine that performs multiplications, we can consider it as a blueprint for a special-purpose computer that will perform multiplications, or rather as a blueprint for the multiplying organ of a computer.

A Turing machine can also be viewed as a computer program whose instructions will be applied by a general-purpose or universal computer. The definitions we gave in § 2.1 can be considered as defining a programming language. In order to be used by a computer, a program must be translated into a corresponding set of computer instructions. This translation is performed by a computer program (called a compiler or an interpreter). We can always describe this translation program by a Turing machine (U). We then have the following picture. A Turing machine (U) is such that its inputs are Turing machines (i.e., programs) together with their relevant data. The machine (U) interprets its inputs and performs the corresponding computations.

It is possible to construct a Turing machine (U) that will perform any computation of any Turing machine. For inputs the machine (U) will have pairs of strings composed of a string $s(T)$ that corresponds to a Turing machine (T) and of a word f, the input to (T). It is possible to give instructions for (U) that will have the following effect. (U) will look at f (beginning with its leftmost letter, say a_1) and then will inspect $s(T)$ to check how f is to be modified [the first step will be to check whether there is a situation (a_1, S_0) corresponding to an instruction of (T), and then to modify f according to the corresponding right member, if any]. (U) will work back and forth between f and $s(T)$, and will possibly block. The final modifications of f provide the result of the computation of f by (T).

2.3.2
GENERALIZATIONS OF TURING MACHINES

More general automata can be defined in terms of the "hardware" we used in defining the Turing machine. We could use, for example:

1. A single central unit that can be assigned a finite number of states.

2. A finite number of heads that can act on a tape in various ways:
   a. by reading, or by writing on it, or by doing both;
   b. by moving the tape only to the left, only to the right, or in both directions.

The number and special nature of the heads determine a situation of the automaton. Given a situation, a finite set of instructions defines the next situation of the automaton. Moreover, initial and final situations can be defined in order to indicate the beginning and the end of a computation.

According to Church's thesis, Turing machines are the most powerful machines that can be defined; so, no matter how many tapes, instructions, and so on an automaton has, there will always exist for it an equivalent Turing machine (i.e., a machine with one reading-writing head that performs exactly the same computations).

Usually the more complicated devices are considered for the definition of restricted classes of computations. Then, special modes of reading-writing are often added to the description of automata. For example, the amount of tape used in a computation can be a fixed function of the length of the input. Another example of restriction consists in having to the left (or to the right) of the reading-writing head a tape with only blank squares.

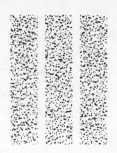

Formal Systems

Rewriting Systems

3.1.1
DEFINITIONS

Formal systems, or rewriting systems, or combinatorial systems are defined by means of:

1. A finite alphabet $V = \{a_i : 0 \leqslant i \leqslant n\}$, which is used to construct strings (i.e., words, or sentences if we call V a vocabulary).

2. A set of words A defined on V: $A \subset VV^*$, which is usually finite. The words of A are called the axioms of the rewriting system.

3. A finite set of productions, or rules, written and interpreted as follows: φ and ψ are words on V, or, more precisely,

$$\varphi \in VV^*, \qquad \psi \in V^*,$$

(φ cannot be the null word). The symbol "arrow" ($\rightarrow \notin V$) is to be read "is rewritten."

Rules modify words of V^*; they replace a segment matched by the left-hand side of the arrow, namely φ, by another segment (i.e., ψ). Let $f \in V^*$. If f has the shape

$$f = \alpha\varphi\beta, \qquad \alpha, \beta \in V^*,$$

the result of the application of the rule $\varphi \rightarrow \psi$ will be a word g such that

$$g = \alpha\psi\beta.$$

The parts α and β are left unchanged. If f does not have the required shape, the rule will not apply.

Languages are defined in the following way. First we apply the rules to the axioms. We get a set of new words to which we apply the rules, and we go on, applying the rules to all new words that are obtained by means of the rules. The set of all words that can be obtained by this process is called the language generated by the system.[1]

Given a formal system (G), a derivation of a word f in (G), starting with the word f_0, is a series

$$f_0, f_1, f_2, \ldots, f_i, \ldots, f_n = f, \qquad f_i \in V^*,$$

such that each f_i, for $1 \leqslant i \leqslant n$, is obtained from f_{i-1} by application of a rule of (G).

The language generated by (G), denoted as $L(G)$, is the set of the words that can be derived in (G), starting all derivations with the axioms (i.e., all f_0's that are in A). A rule, or a series of rules, may be applied any number of times. Such a process allows generating infinite languages by means of finite systems of rules.

EXAMPLE I _____

(G_1) will be composed of a vocabulary of two elements, an axiom, and a rule:

$$V = \{a, c\}, \qquad A = \{c\}, \qquad R = \{c \rightarrow aca\}.$$

All derivations are of the type

$$c \rightarrow aca \rightarrow aacaa \rightarrow \cdots \rightarrow a^n c a^n \rightarrow \cdots$$

The language includes all strings that have an equal number of a's on each side of c, and only these:

$$L(G_1) = \{a^n c a^n : n > 0\}.$$

---

[1] We will consider that the vacuous substitution (i.e., no application of a rule) also applies. This convention allows us to include the axioms in the language of the system.

EXAMPLE II

(G_2) will be composed of

$$V = \{a, b\}, \qquad A = \{ab\}, \qquad R = \{ab \rightarrow abab\}.$$

The derivations are of the type

$$ab \rightarrow abab \rightarrow ababab \rightarrow \cdots \rightarrow (ab)^p \rightarrow \cdots$$

and the language is

$$L(G_2) = \{(ab)^p : p \geqslant 1\}.$$

3.1.2
REWRITING RULES
AND BUILDING PROCESSES

The derivations (namely the rules) of these two examples do not provide the same type of information about the way the sequences are actually constructed. In (G_1) the substitutions are well defined; they all have to occur in the middle of the word, which is marked by c (c does not occur in any other position of a word). In (G_2) the situation is quite different. Except for the axiom, a word of $L(G_2)$ contains more than one sequence ab, and we can interpret the rule by saying that any of these ab's can be duplicated by the rule. For example, when we consider the part of the derivation

$$ababab \rightarrow abababab,$$

we do not know to which of the three ab's of the first member the rule $ab \rightarrow abab$ has applied. Looking at the strings in terms of sequences of

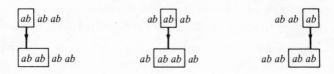

FIGURE 3.1

ab's, we see there are as many ways of applying the rule as there are ab's in the string (Figure 3.1).

There are other ways to look at the effect of the rule

$$ab \rightarrow abab.$$

For example, we can say that the rule inserts ba between a and b. Also, we talked about substitutions: The rule substitutes $abab$ for ab. But we may want to say that the rule appends ab to the right of a sequence ab, or to its left. Such formal properties are sometimes important in the description of linguistic phenomena. They are constantly used in transformational analysis (also in Harris' string analysis). Their description cannot be included directly in our present definition of a rewriting system. We will indicate various extensions of the definitions that will allow us to account in a natural way for the types of building processes just exemplified.

3.1.3
AUXILIARY SYMBOLS

For certain descriptive purposes of the sort just mentioned, it is quite natural to distinguish several types of elements in the alphabet of a rewriting system.

3.1.3.1
NAMES

When a string, or rather a family of strings, behaves within a language in some regular way, which means that the rules that define the language will refer to these strings for various operations, it is convenient to give a name to this family of strings. Names such as "noun," "verb," "adjective," "adverb" are given in traditional grammars to words that exhibit a certain regular behavior. For example, a name such as "noun phrase" (*NP*) can be justified on various grounds.[2] Noun phrases contain nouns that occur, in most of their syntactic positions, together with determiners (definite articles, indefinite articles, and so on), with adjectives, with relative clauses, and so on. It is generally considered that these co-occurrences do not vary much, whether the syntactic position of the noun is subject, direct object, indirect object, and so on.

One also has to relate pairs of sentences of the type

(The man who arrived) gave (a book) to John,
(A book) was given to John by (the man who arrived).

Active and passive sentences are related by some rule (perhaps more than one) that has the effect of exchanging subject and direct object, and of introducing the auxiliary *be* and the preposition *by*. The rule is such that it refers to the noun phrases found in subject and object positions. If the rule applied only to nouns, we would obtain incorrect strings such as

*Book was given a to John by (the man who arrived),

in which the noun *book* has been moved, but not its article *a*. Also there are sets of sentences such as

(1)   *(The man who arrived) gave (a book) (to John),*

---

[2] The set of all *NP*'s (described in terms of sequences of English words) is infinite. The fact that an *NP* may contain a relative clause, and that a relative clause in turn may contain an *NP*, allows unbounded length. The grammatical properties of noun phrases do not depend, in general, on their content or on their length.

(2) *It is (the man who arrived) that gave a book to John,*

(3) *It is (a book) that the man who arrived gave to John,*

(4) *It is (to John) that the man who arrived gave a book.*

The sentences (2), (3), and (4) can be derived from the string

It is that (1)

by a rule that takes certain noun phrases of (1) (here subject, direct and indirect objects) and moves them between *is* and *that*. Again, if this rule did
not refer to the entire *NP*, it would produce sequences that are not gram-
matically correct—as in the following, where *the man* has been moved, but its
relative clause has been left behind:

*It is the man that who arrived gave a book to John.

These observations demonstrate the special behavior of certain sequences,
and justify that a name be given to them.

In describing English, besides a terminal vocabulary V_T composed of
morphemes and words, we must also use an auxiliary vocabulary V_A composed of symbols (abstract entities) necessary for capturing regularities and
generalizations about linguistic facts. The auxiliary vocabulary will contain
symbols such as V for "verb," N for "noun," *NP* for "noun phrase," and so
on.

Definition

**For a formal system whose alphabet is divided into auxiliary and terminal symbols,
the generated language will be the set of all terminal strings (i.e., strings on the terminal
alphabet) that can be derived from the axioms.**

3.1.3.2
OTHER USES

Auxiliary symbols may also help to specify the way certain families of strings
are built. The formal system

$$V_T = \{a, b\}, \quad V_A = \{S\}, \quad A = \{S\}, \quad R = \{S \to abS, S \to ab\}$$

defines the same language as in Example II above:

$$L(G_2) = \{(ab)^p : p \geqslant 1\}.$$

Here, the symbol S indicates the location where a new *ab* is to be added by a
rule of R. Because this process is right branching, we avoid most of the

ambiguities of interpretation that we had with the rule $ab \to abab$. Auxiliary symbols also allow a "better control" of the derivation of sequences. In our new system, we have derivations of the type

$$S \to abS \to ababS \to abababS \to abababab.$$

The rule $S \to abS$ has been applied three times, and the rule $S \to ab$ once. After this last rule has been applied, we have reached a sequence of the language, and there is no rule that applies any further. We will call such last rules terminal or lexical rules, and will say that the derivations have blocked. Notice that with the rule $ab \to abab$ derivations never block. On the other hand, it is possible to have formal systems, such as

$$V_T = \{a, b\}, \quad V_A = \{S, T\}, \quad A = \{S\}, \quad \{R = S \to abS, S \to abT\}$$

with derivations that never terminate. In such cases the generated language is empty.[3]

Auxiliary symbols, and also terminal symbols, may be used as markers for indicating various types of boundaries. In Example I the symbol c was a boundary that indicated the middle of the word. In linguistics the symbol $\#$ is often used as a morpheme or sentence boundary.

Consider, for example, the two sentences

(S₁) The man sold a book,

(S₂) The man arrived.

There are grammar rules that can apply within (S_1) or within (S_2). The passive rule may apply to (S_1), yielding

A book was sold by the man.

Pronoun formation may apply to (S_2), yielding

He arrived.

On the other hand, there are rules that operate on pairs such as $[(S_1), (S_2)]$. Relative clause formation applied to the product $(S_1)(S_2)$:

The man sold a book the man arrived

yields

The man who arrived sold a book.

---

[3] Notice that an empty language (i.e., empty set) is different from the language that contains only the empty or null word e. The latter is not empty since it contains the word e.

But the passive rule has to be defined in such a way that it also applies to the sentences

The man sold a book to a man

or

The man sold a man a book.

Since both the passive rule and the relative clause rule belong to the grammar of English, we have nothing to prevent the passive rule from applying to $(S_1)(S_2)$, yielding a string such as

*A man was sold a book by the man arrived

which is not a sentence. Since the two sentences (S_1), (S_2) were simply concatenated, the passive rule was able to apply across sentences. Of course, such a grammar is inadequate. In order to avoid the defect that we just indicated, we need a special symbol $\#$ for sentence boundary, and then we formulate the passive rule in such a way that it applies only to strings of the type $\# S \#$—that is, it applies only within sentence boundaries. In the same way, relative clause formation would apply to strings of the type $\# S \# S \#$—across sentence boundaries.[4]

3.1.4
VARIABLES

For certain descriptive purposes, it is of interest to leave the shape of whole families of strings completely unspecified. We can then use certain symbols $(W, X, Y, \ldots)$ that do not belong to either the auxiliary or terminal alphabet of the system. Consider, for example, the following type of trans-formations performed on any string defined on the alphabet $\{a, b, c\}$ that begins with an a and ends with an a: The rightmost a has to be brought next to the leftmost one.

We can use the "rule"

$$a X a \rightarrow a a X$$

which means that any string of the shape $a X a$, where X can be any element of $\{a, b, c\}^*$, is rewritten as $aa X$. With respect to the definitions of formal systems that we gave, the X of such a "rule" would not belong to the terminal or auxiliary alphabet. Rather, X is a variable ranging over any string on

---

[4] Many other refinements are necessary for these two rules to apply correctly. We have indicated only a first step toward a general solution.

$\{a, b, c\}$. Translating the "rule" $a\,X\,a \to aa\,X$ in terms of rules of a rewriting system could lead us to an infinite number of rules, since we would have to replace X by all strings in $\{a, b, c\}$.

Another example is the "rule"

$$X \to X\,X, \qquad \text{where } X \text{ ranges over } \{a, b, c\}^*,$$

which takes any string X and duplicates it.

Such devices are called *rule schemata*. They are used in many applications of formal systems as a shorthand for sets of rules, and at the same time they represent adequately, and in natural ways, combinatorial processes. In the examples above we could replace each of the rule schemata by a finite set of rules using auxiliary symbols. They would have the same effect, but the essence of the process (permutation, duplication) would no longer be as apparent.

Variables are also used in grammatical descriptions. Consider the case of certain *who*-questions. The following data are to be accounted for.

(1) $\begin{cases} \textit{Mary saw someone.} \\ \textit{Whom did Mary see?} \end{cases}$

(2) $\begin{cases} \textit{He believed Mary saw someone.} \\ \textit{Whom did he believe Mary saw?} \end{cases}$

There are many reasons to relate declarative sentences containing the indefinite pronoun *someone* to *who*-questions (for example, the co-occurrence with the particle *else*). Pair (1) suggests that *someone*, direct object of *saw*, main verb of the sentence, is replaced by *whom* and moved to the left of the string.[5] Pair (2) shows that *someone* does not have to be the direct object of the main verb of the whole sentence but can be the direct object of the main verb of a sentential complement. We can have sentences with more than two verbs as in (2); auxiliaries, modals, verbs such as *to try to*, *to like*, and so on can be inserted in (2). In all cases the rule pattern is the same: The direct object of the last verb is replaced by *whom* and moved to the left of the whole sentence. This transformation can be written

$$\# \; NP \; t \; V \; X \; someone \; \#$$

$$\to \; \# \; Whom \; t \; NP \; V \; X \; ? \; \#$$

NP and *V* are respectively the subject and the verb of the main sentence; *t* is a tense marker or a modal. When *t* is an affix (-*ed*, -*s*), the auxiliary *do* is introduced and the affix attached to it.

---

[5] Besides replacement and permutation rules, the question transformation involves introduction of *do*, subject inversion, intonation placement, and so on.

The variable X can range over a rather wide variety of sequences. It is sharply distinguished from an auxiliary symbol by the fact that it never corresponds to any grammatical category, or to any sequence that could be given, in a simple way, a name in terms of grammatical categories.

However, in this case there are restrictions on X. For example, the *who*-question rule may not apply to the sentence

He believed the girl who saw someone.

It would yield

*Whom did he believe the girl who saw?

We observe here a restriction on the variable X. It cannot range over strings that cover parts of relative clauses. This use of variable runs into many difficulties,[6] but it has become a standard device in syntax.

3.1.5
EXTENSIONS OF REWRITING SYSTEMS

Various types of systems have been defined, mostly for use in mathematical logic. We give here the most common definitions.

Formal systems are all defined on some alphabet A, and a set of axioms is distinguished in A^*. The notions of derivation and of language are defined as usual.

What we have been calling formal or combinatorial systems are in fact restricted. These terms also apply to rules other than rewriting rules such as

$$\varphi \to \psi.$$

Systems with rules $\varphi \to \psi$ are also called semi-Thue systems. When a system contains the rules $\varphi_i \to \psi_i$, and for each i the rule $\psi_i \to \varphi_i$, it is called a Thue system. In other words, the rules are not oriented and are defined by unordered pairs $\{\varphi_i, \psi_i\}$. These rules are also written $\varphi_i \Leftrightarrow \psi_i$, the double arrow indicating the symmetry. These systems perform substitutions of strings.

A system with rules of the type

$$\varphi X \to X\psi$$

---

[6] For a discussion of some of these problems, cf. J. R. Ross, "Variables in Syntax," Ph.D. Thesis, M.I.T., 1967.

where X is a variable (ranging over the part not represented by φ and for all the words in the alphabet) is called a normal system. Each rule performs at the same time a substitution and a permutation: The leftmost part φ of a word is replaced by ψ and put to the right of the unchanged part X. If we replace $\rightarrow$ by the double arrow, we have a Post system. The rules of a Post system all have the form $\varphi X \Leftrightarrow X\psi$.

*3.2

Algebraic Systems

We consider now a set of rules of the Thue type

$$\{\varphi_i \rightarrow \psi_i, \psi_i \rightarrow \varphi_i; \ 1 \leqslant i \leqslant m\}, \ \varphi_i, \psi_i \in V^*,$$

which we shall write as

$$\{\varphi_i \leftrightarrow \psi_i : 1 \leqslant i \leqslant m\}.$$

Instead of considering derivations that start with a set of axioms and that define a language, we will only be concerned with the study of derivations that can link any pair of words on V.

Given two arbitrary words $f_r, f_s \in V^*$, if there exists a derivation that links them, we will write

$$f_r \Leftrightarrow f_s.$$

The symbol $\Leftrightarrow$ therefore defines a relation on V^*.

3.2.1
THE EQUIVALENCE RELATION $\Leftrightarrow$

Property 1

The relation $\Leftrightarrow$ is an equivalence relation.

The relation $\Leftrightarrow$ is
1. Symmetrical; the expression

$$f_r \Leftrightarrow f_s$$

means that

$$(1) \quad f_t \rightarrow f_t \rightarrow \cdots \rightarrow f_s.$$

Each arrow $\rightarrow$ corresponds to a rule $\varphi_i \rightarrow \psi_i$. By applying all the corresponding symmetrical rules $\psi_i \rightarrow \varphi_i$, we can reverse the derivation (1), which yields

(2) $f_s \rightarrow \cdots \rightarrow f_t \rightarrow f_r$

—that is to say,

$f_s \Leftrightarrow f_r,$

2. Reflexive; we have

$f_r \Leftrightarrow f_r$

by a convention about vacuous application of rules.
3. Transitive; if $f_r \Leftrightarrow f_s$ and $f_s \Leftrightarrow f_t$, then, by adjoining the derivation of f_t from f_s to the right of the first derivation, we have

$f_r \Leftrightarrow f_t.$

As with any equivalence relation, we obtain a partition of V^* into disjoint equivalence classes: All words that can be linked by a derivation, and only these, belong to the same class. We will now show that the relation $\Leftrightarrow$ has further algebraic properties.

3.2.2
THE CONGRUENCE RELATION $\Leftrightarrow$

D e f i n i t i o n

A relation R defined on products of elements (here on strings over an alphabet V) is right invariant if, when $x R y$ $(x, y \in V^*)$, we have (for each $u \in V^*$) $x u R y u$; R is left invariant if, for all u's, $u x R u y$.
    A relation R is a congruence relation, if it is both right and left invariant—that is, if $x R y$ $(x, y \in V^*)$ implies that for all u's and v's $(\in V^*)$ we have $u x v R u y v$.

P r o p e r t y 2

The relation $\Leftrightarrow$ is a congruence relation.
    Let us consider four words f_1, f_2, g_1, g_2 such that

$f_1 \Leftrightarrow f_2$ and $g_1 \Leftrightarrow g_2.$

We have $f_1 g_1 \Leftrightarrow f_2 g_1$ (for any $g_1 \in V^*$), since adjoining g_1 to the right of f_1

does not affect the derivation of f_1 to f_2. In the same way, we have

$$f_2 g_1 \Leftrightarrow f_2 g_2 \qquad \text{(for any } f_2 \in V^*).$$

The relation $\Leftrightarrow$, being both left and right invariant, is a congruence relation.

3.2.3
THE PRODUCT OF CLASSES

Combining $f_1 g_1 \Leftrightarrow f_2 g_1$ and $f_2 g_1 \Leftrightarrow f_2 g_2$ provides $f_1 g_1 \Leftrightarrow f_2 g_2$, which indicates the following situation. Let $[f]$ be the equivalence class of f_1 (and of f_2), $[g]$ the equivalence class of g_1 (and of g_2). When we concatenate f_1 and g_1 on the one hand, and f_2 and g_2 on the other, the class of $f_1 g_1$ is the same as the class of $f_2 g_2$. For any f_i and g_i chosen in $[f]$ and $[g]$, respectively, the product $f_i g_i$ is in a fixed class that we call $[fg]$. We have a correspondence between the two classes $[f]$, $[g]$ on one side and the single class $[fg]$ on the other. We are justified in writing it as a product: $[f][g] = [fg]$.

Property

The product of classes is associative.

We have to show that if $[f]$, $[g]$, $[h]$ are equivalence classes, the product is such that

$$[f]([g][h]) = ([f][g])[h].$$

Let us consider the expression $([f][g])[h]$. We can replace in it $[f][g]$ by the corresponding product $[fg]$, and we have

$$([f][g])[h] = [fg][h].$$

In the same way we can multiply $[fg]$ and $[h]$, obtaining

$$([f][g])[h] = [fg][h] = [fgh].$$

Since concatenation is associative, we can write

$$[fgh] = [f(gh)] \quad \text{—i.e.,} \quad = [f][gh]$$

and

$$[gh] = [g][h].$$

which proves that

$$([f][g])[h] = [fgh] = ([f])([g][h]).$$

We obtain the following system. Starting with the set V^* of all strings on V, and with a finite set of rewriting rules, we defined a relation that divides V^* into nonoverlapping classes (lefthand side of Figure 3.2). Now we can look at the classes as elements of a set M (righthand side of Figure 3.2). The correspondence between V^* and M is indicated by arrows.

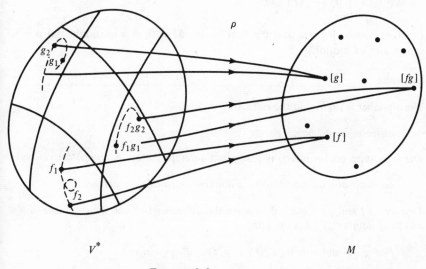

FIGURE 3.2

The words which are linked by dotted lines are related by a derivation. These lines cannot cross the class boundaries (solid lines).

3.2.4
MORPHISM

The arrows between V^* and M define a mapping that will be called ρ and that has the following property: For all $f, g \in V^*$, we have

$$\rho(f)\,\rho(g) = [f][g] = [fg] = \rho(fg)$$

The mapping ρ is then a morphism that operates between two associative structures (i.e., two sets on which an associative product is defined): V^*, which is a free monoid, and M.

When we defined the rules of the system, we had

$$\varphi_i, \psi_i \in V^*.$$

which implies that we can have rules of the forms $\varphi_i \rightarrow e$ and $e \rightarrow \varphi_i$. The restriction $\varphi_i \in VV^*$ that we imposed on rewriting systems was not essential. The null word e can then have a class $[e]$ in exactly the same way as any other word, and we have

$$[f][e] = [fe] = [f],$$
$$[e][f] = [ef] = [f].$$

In other terms, $[e]$ is a unit element in M. M is then a monoid, and ρ is a morphism of monoids.

The alphabet is $\{a, b\}$ and the rules are

$$ab \Leftrightarrow e \quad \text{and} \quad ba \Leftrightarrow e.$$

The rules suppress (or insert) two adjacent different letters. A typical derivation is

$$aaababababbbb \Leftrightarrow aaababbbb \Leftrightarrow aaabbbb \Leftrightarrow aabbb \Leftrightarrow abb \Leftrightarrow b.$$

Two words f and g are equivalent when the difference between their number of a's and their number of b's is the same:

$$f \Leftrightarrow g \quad \text{if and only if} \quad d_a^0(f) - d_b^0(f) = d_e^0(g) - d_b^0(g).$$

This relation gives a clear picture of the equivalence classes of $\{a, b\}^*$. First, we can notice that the class of e is composed of all words that have the same number of a's and b's. Second, the classes are in one-to-one correspondence with the integers. The monoid of the classes is then isomorphic to the additive group of the integers.

Converse Property

We have just proved that given a finite set of rules $\varphi \rightarrow \psi$ defined over V^*, we can divide V^* into a set of equivalence classes that constitutes a monoid obtained from V^* by morphism. We now show that given a free monoid V^*, and a morphic monoid $M = \rho(V^*)$, the morphism ρ determines a congruence relation over V^*.

Let us consider the relation R between words of V^*: f_1 and f_2 in V^* are in relation R when they have the same morphic image in M:

$$f_1 \, R \, f_2 \quad \text{when} \quad \rho(f_1) = \rho(f_2)$$

It is easy to verify that R is an equivalence relation, the classes being composed of all words that have the same image under ρ.

Let u, v be two arbitrary words of V^*, and let us consider the words $u f_1 v$ and $u f_2 v$. By definition of the morphism ρ we have

$$\rho(u f_1 v) = \rho(u)\rho(f_1)\rho(v),$$
$$\rho(u f_2 v) = \rho(u)\rho(f_2)\rho(v).$$

Since for all pairs of strings f_1, f_2 in relation R we have $\rho(f_1) = \rho(f_2)$, we also have

$$\rho(u)\rho(f_1)\rho(v) = \rho(u)\rho(f_2)\rho(v)$$

or

$$\rho(u f_1 v) = \rho(u f_2 v)$$

or, in terms of R,

$$u f_1 v \, R \, u f_2 v,$$

which shows that R is a congruence relation.

3.2.5
REMARKS

The only real difference between rewriting systems (with rules $\varphi \rightarrow \psi$) and algebraic systems arises from the choice of a set of axioms from which a language is derived. In terms of an algebraic system, a language will be a union of equivalence classes, which is just the same as choosing a set of axioms, since the union of the classes of the axioms constitutes the language.

Our example suggests the interest of formulating definitions of languages in algebraic terms. We noticed that the rules had the effect of dividing V^* into classes that are isomorphic to the additive group of the integers. A language is a union of classes; it corresponds to a subset of the additive group—that is, to a special set of integers. The study of integers is an important part of mathematics, and many important and powerful tools are available for it. We can use some of these tools to perform studies on families of strings. We will mention later certain results of this type (algebraic characterization of Kleene's languages, Schützenberger's characterization of context-free languages).

Relations Between
Turing Machines
and Rewriting Systems

Church's thesis states that all the devices that
formalize the intuitive notion of computability are
equivalent. We present here various relations
between Turing machines and rewriting systems.

Turing Machines
and Rewriting Systems

We have seen that Turing machines and formal systems can be used
for defining languages—that is, for characterizing certain subsets L of some
set (free monoid) V^*. We have also seen that we can use these devices for
describing specific building processes. We now study more precisely the
relations between these two classes of devices.

We noted that the class of languages characterizable by Turing machines
is denumerably infinite; the same is true of rewriting systems. A rewriting
system is defined by

1. a set of axioms:

$$A = \{f_i : 1 \leqslant i \leqslant m\}, \qquad f_i \in V_V^*,$$

2. a set of rules:

$$R = \{\varphi_j \to \psi_j : 1 \leqslant j \leqslant n\}, \qquad \varphi_j, \psi_j \in V^*.$$

We can write these sets in the form of a string. Using the separator $\#$, we have, for example,

(FS) $f_1 \# f_2 \# \cdots \# f_m \# \varphi_1 \to \psi_1 \# \cdots \# \varphi_n \to \psi_n \#.$

This string is defined on the alphabet $V \cup \{\to, \#\}$. It is a finite string, since A and R are finite.[1]

Since to any formal system we can associate a finite string of unbounded length, the set of all formal system is denumerably infinite, and we are in the same situation as with Turing machines. The set of all possible languages on a finite alphabet is nondenumerable, so formal systems can serve to describe only a certain restricted class of languages. We have on the one hand the class of languages definable by Turing machines, what we have called recursively enumerable languages, and on the other hand the class of languages definable by formal systems. It is interesting to see how these two classes are related. Is one of them included in the other, are they disjoint, or do they intersect? We will show in §§ 4.2 and 4.3 that each is included in the other—that is, they are identical. In other words, when a language is

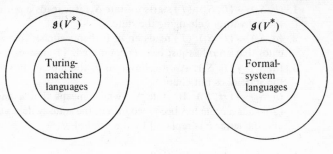

FIGURE 4.1

$\mathfrak{F}(V^*)$ is the set of all languages of the alphabet V—that is, the set of all subsets of V^*. For Turing-machine languages (which we have also called recursively enumerable languages) and formal-system languages we have the two pictures above. The problem is to compare the two subsets of $\mathfrak{F}(V^*)$.

[1] The set of all formal systems is given by the expression

$$(V V^* \#)^*((V^* \to V^*) \#)^*.$$

A formal system is determined by choosing an alphabet V and one element of the corresponding set of formal systems.

definable by means of a formal system, it is also definable by a Turing machine, and vice versa. Moreover, we will see that given either of the two devices, it is possible to construct effectively the other.

4.2

Turing Machines for Substitutions

We shall now see how to build effectively a Turing machine that performs a substitution in a string, replacing some specified substring by some other given sequence.

Let V be the alphabet of the machine (T); let φ and ψ be two words on V [$\varphi \in VV^*$ (i.e., φ is not null), $\psi \in V^*$]. If f is an input to (T), machine (T) will check whether substring φ occurs in f (i.e., whether $f = \alpha\varphi\beta$). If it occurs, (T) will then replace φ by ψ.

EXAMPLE _____

$$V = \{a, b\}, \quad \varphi = ab, \quad \psi = a$$

The machine (T) that will substitute a for ab in any sequence of a's and b's has the following instructions.

1. $(b, S_0) \rightarrow (L, S_0)$: (T) starts in state S_0; if it reads a b it moves the tape to the left without changing the state.
2. $(a, S_0) \rightarrow (L, S_1)$: (T) reads an a; it then switches to a state S_1 that indicates that an a has just been encountered. (T) moves the tape to the left.
3. $(a, S_1) \rightarrow (L, S_1)$: An a follows an a, the tape is moved to the left, and the state does not change.
4. $(b, S_1) \rightarrow (\#, S_2)$: In state S_1, which means that a has just been read, (T) reads a b; ab has been recognized, the state switches to a new value S_2, and the letter b is replaced by the symbol $\#$.

In this case we started with the tape

α	a	b	β

$\alpha \notin V^* ab\, V^*$,

and ended with

α	a	$\#$	β

If, by a special convention, we ignore the blank symbol $\#$, we can consider that the substitution $ab \rightarrow a$ has been applied. However, this is a very special case. We took advantage of the fact that erasing b in ab or substituting a for ab are equivalent operations. This is by no means a general procedure. If φ and ψ are unrelated in shape, which is the general case, we need instead of the single state S_1 sequences of states that will be used to remember φ. In the same way, instead of the single state S_2 we will use sequences of states that remember ψ.

Several other observations must be made. First, we might consider that the result of the preceding substitution ought to be the tape

α	a	β

—that is, no blank should occur within the segment of the tape where the substitution is applied. With this definition, we will have to add to the instructions of (T) new instructions that will move each letter of the sequence $\beta \in \{a, b\}^*$ one square to the left. The following instructions will perform this adjustment:

$$(\#, S_2) \rightarrow (L, S_3)$$
$$\left.\begin{array}{l} (a, S_3) \rightarrow (\#, S_{ra}) \\ (b, S_3) \rightarrow (\#, S_{rb}) \end{array}\right\} \text{ States } S_{ra} \text{ and } S_{rb} \text{ remember } a \text{ and } b \text{, respectively}$$
$$(\#, S_{ra}) \rightarrow (R, S_{wa})$$
$$(\#, S_{rb}) \rightarrow (R, S_{wb})$$
$$\left.\begin{array}{l} (\#, S_{wa}) \rightarrow (a, S_4) \\ (\#, S_{wb}) \rightarrow (b, S_4) \end{array}\right\} \text{ States } S_{wa} \text{ and } S_{wb} \text{ are used to write } a \text{ and } b \text{ on the tape}$$
$$(a, S_4) \rightarrow (L, S_2)$$
$$(b, S_4) \rightarrow (L, S_2).$$

If the right member ψ of the substitution rule $\varphi \rightarrow \psi$ were longer than φ, then not enough squares would be immediately available on the tape. Starting from

α	φ	β

, in order to obtain

α	ψ	β

,

β would have to be moved $|\psi| - |\varphi|$ squares to the right. The preceding set of instructions could easily be generalized to shift β over a fixed number k of blanks.

Our substitution instructions have a peculiarity. Suppose that we have as an input word to (T) the sequence *baabaaba*; the result can only be *baaaaba*, where only the leftmost occurrence of *ab* has been substituted. The example just outlined is one of a Turing machine that performs on a word a single substitution that applies only once, for a given rule $\varphi \rightarrow \psi$. But according to the rewriting rule *ab* $\rightarrow$ *a* we have three possible results for the string *baabaaba*, since this string contains two occurrences of *ab*:

> *baaaaba*,   application to the leftmost occurrence of *ab*, which is what
> (T) does
> *baabaaa*   application to the rightmost occurrence of *ab*
> *baaaaa*   both applications of the rule.

One could build Turing machines that would perform each of the other two modes of substitution.

It is always possible to define a Turing machine that will substitute strings in any predetermined way, and in particular to obtain any result that could be obtained by means of a rewriting rule. It is easy to replicate the construction that we outlined for any finite set R of rewriting rules and to gather the computing instructions into a unique Turing machine. Then, in order to define a language, we can adopt the following convention: All computations will start with a finite set A of words or with a word on which a substitution has been performed (this will be easy to realize in a non-deterministic way). The resulting Turing machine simulates all the derivations of a rewriting system of axioms A and rules R.

4.3

Formal Systems
Simulating Turing Machines

The pattern presented by a Turing machine at each step of the computation can be described by means of a string. We insert on the tape, and to the

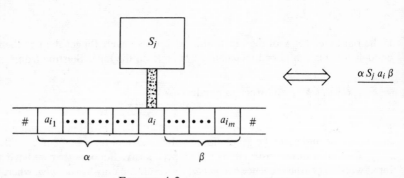

FIGURE 4.2

left of the symbol appearing under the head of the machine, a symbol that indicates the state of the machine (Figure 4.2). The string $\alpha\, S_j\, a_i\, \beta$ corresponds to a Turing machine in state S_j, with a tape $\alpha\, a_i\, \beta$, where a_i is under the reading head. In a string, in general, we ignore the subparts that are filled with blanks, though we do not do so in a tape. Given a Turing machine (T), with each of its instructions of the type

$$(a_i, S_j) \rightarrow (a_k, S_l)$$

we will associate the rewriting rule

(I$_1$) $S_j a_i \rightarrow S_l a_k$

that modifies the lefthand string exactly as the Turing machine does for its tape.

In the same way, with each instruction

$(a_i, S_j) \rightarrow (L, S_l)$

we associate a rule

(I$_2$) $S_j\, a_i \rightarrow a_i\, S_j,$

and with each instruction

$(a_i, S_j) \rightarrow (R, S_l)$

we have to associate the set of rules

(I$_3$) $a_k\, S_j\, a_i \rightarrow S_j\, a_k\, a_i,$

where a_k, the rightmost symbol of α, can be any element of the alphabet.[2]

Let us now compare the ways in which a Turing machine and its associated rewriting system characterize a given language. The Turing machine is given a string on its alphabet; starting in state S_0 with its head on the leftmost symbol of the string, it performs a computation. If the computation ever comes to an end (and only then), the string belongs to the language. On the other hand, the associated system has computation rules that simulate the action of the machine. The way these rules were defined from the instructions guarantees that they have the same effect as the machine. The only parts of the computation that are not quite clear are the starting and ending points.

Since any word of V^* can be placed on the tape of the machine, and since these words correspond to the axioms of the rewriting system, we will introduce an axiom named A, and the rules

(II) $\begin{cases} A \rightarrow A\, a_i & \text{for } a_i \in V \\ A \rightarrow S_0\, a_i & \text{for } a_i \in V \end{cases}$

These rules generate all sequences on V with S_0 as a prefix—that is, all initial configurations of the Turing machines. On these strings the other rules defined for the system will apply.

---

[2] We can also have $a_k = \#$.

The rewriting system uses two categories of symbols—on the one hand, V, which constitutes the terminal alphabet, and on the other hand, the set $\{A, S_i; 0 \leqslant i \leqslant N\}$ [N is the number of states of the machine (T)] that has to be looked at as a nonterminal alphabet. In order to generate a terminal language, one has to eliminate from the strings any auxiliary symbol. In order to generate the language defined by (T), we have to eliminate any S_i from strings of the shape $V^* S_i a_j V^*$ and such that (a_i, S_j) is not a situation of (T) [i.e., strings resulting from a terminated computation of (T)].

We next add to the associated rewriting system the rules

(III) $S_i a_j \rightarrow a_j$

for all pairs (i, j) such that (a_i, S_j) is not a situation of (T).

It is now clear that the rewriting system that has A as a set of axioms, and (I_1), (I_2), (I_3), (II), (III) for rules, characterizes exactly the language characterized by T. However, this system does not generate the language according to the definitions, since we should obtain x (the string that belongs to the language) at the last step of the derivation. The rewriting rules use x as a starting string and modify it. In order to keep an intact copy of x, we have to modify the system. We modify the shape of rules (III). They will all be of the form $S_i a_j \rightarrow n a_j$, where n is a new marker (not in V). Instead of (II) we will have rules that generate strings of the form $p S_0 x m x$, $x \in V^*$, where p is a punctuation mark and m is a special marker that separates the two copies of the input string x. All computations will be performed between n and m by the rules (I_1), (I_2), (I_3). Then we add the new rules: $n a_j \rightarrow n$, $a_j n \rightarrow n$ for all a_j's, and the rule $p n m \rightarrow e$. These rules suppress all remainders of the computation just in case x was in the language of (T). This new system generates exactly the language of (T). We now have the result:

Formal systems and Turing machines characterize the same family of languages, namely the class of recursively enumerable languages.[3]

4.4

Flow Charts

Turing machines and rewriting systems may be used to describe any computation. There are other ways of stating algorithms. One that is commonly

---

[3] We did not give here any proof of this equivalence, but our outline of a proof is essentially correct. As an exercise the reader should try to supply the missing parts. For a rigorous proof of this property cf. M. Davis, *Computability and Unsolvability* (New York: McGraw-Hill, Inc., 1958).

used is the flow chart, of which we shall give an example to suggest the kind of apparatus involved.

Consider the Turing machine defined by the states $\Sigma = \{S_0, S_1, S_f\}$, the alphabet $A = \{\#, a, b\}$, and the rules

(1) $(a, S_0) \rightarrow (L, S_0)$

(2) $(b, S_0) \rightarrow (L, S_1)$

(3) $(b, S_1) \rightarrow (L, S_1)$

(4) $(\#, S_0) \rightarrow (L, S_f)$

(5) $(\#, S_1) \rightarrow (L, S_f)$.

This machine characterizes the language $L = \{a^p b^q : p, q \geqslant 0\}$. Starting in the initial state S_0 on the leftmost letter of the string f, it will skip all beginning a's by instruction (1). Instruction (2), by switching to state S_1, remembers that the string is to be checked for the presence of a sequence of b's, which is done by instruction (3). Then the machine will accept the input f (i.e., will block in S_f on the right of f) only if f has the required shape.

A flow chart is a graph composed of instructions inside boxes and linked by arrows that show the order in which the instructions apply. We shall use three kinds of boxes.

1. Square boxes with outgoing arrows indicate computations.

2. Square boxes without outgoing arrows state results.

3. Oval boxes contain questions asked about the computation. From each of these oval boxes two arrows tagged with the two possible answers "yes" or "no" lead to boxes of any type.

A flow chart always refers to some computing mechanism that performs the instructions given in the boxes.[4]

The flow chart in Figure 4.3 is equivalent to the previous Turing machine. It verifies whether f, an input string written on a tape, is in L or not. The computing mechanism is a machine that moves the tape under a reading head one square to the left at a time. The computation starts in the upper box, with the reading head on the leftmost letter of f (or on $\#$ if $f = e$).

[4] Computer analysts use flow charts mainly for stating algorithms that are to be programmed. A much more formal theory of flow charts has been devised by A. A. Markov [*Theory of Algorithms* (Jerusalem: Academic Press, 1961)].

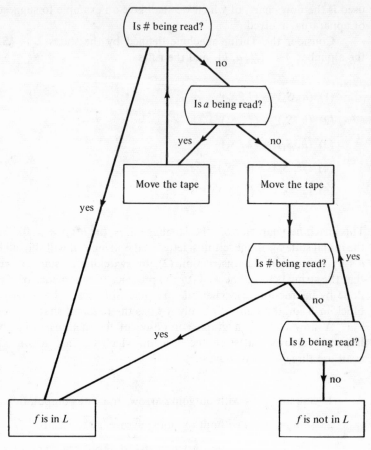

FIGURE 4.3

4.5

Generation Versus Recognition

When we used rewriting systems for characterizing languages, we interpreted
the mechanism in a special way. Starting from an axiom, we applied rules
that could lead to words of the corresponding language; to put it differently,
we built or produced words. We could just as well have applied the following
procedure. Given a word f on the terminal alphabet of a rewriting system
$\langle A, R \rangle$ (A is the set of axioms and R is the set of rules), we look inside the
given word for the occurrence of a right member ψ of a rule $\varphi \to \psi \in R$ of the
system; if we locate such a ψ we replace it by φ. On such a resulting string f_i

we perform the same operation, the result of which is f_{i-1}, and we repeat such steps until we arrive at a string f_0 that is an axiom of the system: $f_0 \in A$.

Such a procedure can be conceived as a recognition procedure. It uses the same apparatus $\langle A, R \rangle$ as the generation procedure did. However, this terminology is only superficially adequate. To define recognition procedure properly, one needs extra procedures not provided by $\langle A, R \rangle$. Suppose, for example, that f (or any f_i) has two factorizations

$$f = \alpha_1 \, \psi_1 \, \beta_1 = \alpha_2 \, \psi_2 \, \beta_2 \qquad \text{(where } \psi_1 = \psi_2 = \psi\text{)}$$

which are such that only one replacement of ψ by φ is possible (i.e., because ψ_1 and ψ_2 overlap) (Figure 4.4).

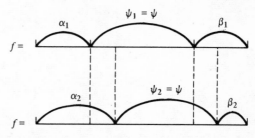

FIGURE 4.4

The word and the rewriting system can be such that when ψ_1 is replaced, the recognition computation never results in an element of A, while when ψ_2 is replaced, the computation leads to an axiom. Similar situations are quite common, showing that all possible paths of a recognition computation have to be explored. This requirement forces us to add to the procedure we gave a bookkeeping device that will avoid entering a given path more than once (or a limited number of times) and will guarantee that all paths are explored. This full recognition procedure does not always exist. We know that for recursively enumerable languages that are not recursive, such a device cannot be built. Notice, however, that we can still give to the rules the "recognition" interpretation. We have also seen that a Turing machine, by performing substitution, could "generate" strings as well as "recognize" them (§ 4.2).

In fact the devices that have been presented (Turing machines and rewriting systems) are neutral with respect to recognition and production. They only "characterize" languages, or "generate" them in the sense that the term "generate" is used in mathematics (e.g., generators of a group, generating function). The notations that we used (such as the arrow) could have been reversed, allowing for other interpretations. It should be clear, however, that the different interpretations correspond mainly to terminological changes, and in order to build actual devices that produce and recognize the strings of a language, we must define other mechanisms.

We recall here that algebraic systems are equivalent to rewriting systems, thus to Turing machines. With algebraic systems, however, the terminology (monoids, generators, equivalence classes) does not lend itself to mechanistic interpretations that are ambiguous. In many ways the algebraic terminology is minimal. It is clearly so with regards to the notion "characterization of a language."

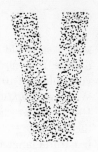

Computing Systems
and Natural Languages

All the concepts we have described so far—Turing
machines, rewriting systems, recursively enumerable
languages, recursive languages—although applicable
to anything that is computable, have a precise
significance with respect to linguistic phenomena.

Natural Languages as
Recursively Enumerable Sets

In Chapter I we recognized that natural languages are discrete and thus can
be looked upon as sets of strings. We also noticed that they constitute
infinite sets, but the processes by which they become infinite (conjunction,
relativization, and so on) are of a finite nature. It is always a few rules
reapplicable indefinitely that make natural languages infinite. As a consequence, linguists can give descriptions in notations of finite size. In other
words they can give descriptions in terms of algorithms.

This situation should not be taken for granted, and we could conceive
of entirely different settings for linguistics. For example, natural languages
could have combinatorial properties such that the number of all possible

sentences would be finite, but so large that it might have to be considered as infinite and nondenumerable. Let us consider a language defined on a vocabulary of 10,000 words (which is a small number for a natural language). We now suppose that all sentences have a length smaller than or equal to 100, and that one-tenth of all possible combinations of words may occur in the language (to allow for restrictions on co-occurrence as they are observed in natural languages). The number of all possible sentences is finite then, but it is of the magnitude of 10^{400}—a number much larger than the number of elementary particles in the whole universe. Yet, although the universe is finite, physicists have found it to be more easily described as being infinite. The regular mathematical tools in physics deal with nondenumerable sets. At first sight the situation could have been the same in linguistics, but many observations about language forced linguists to adopt for their description the general framework of finite systems of the types that we present here. In this sense, it is already a very strong restriction that is observed about the nature of language.

5.2

Special Properties
of Natural Languages

We have concluded that natural languages must be considered recursively enumerable sets. But recursively enumerable sets are of such generality that in most cases their properties are completely irrelevant to the properties that can be observed for natural languages. One of the problems of linguistics is to find formal properties that will be universal (applicable to all natural languages), and that will characterize natural languages as special recursively enumerable sets. The restrictions should eliminate properties that are never observed. For example, the set of prime integers is recursively enumerable (in fact recursive). On the other hand, no natural language has ever been found to contain strings whose length would always be a prime number; thus such sets must be ruled out as possible models for natural languages. Grammars may have other uses than characterizing certain families of strings. They also take part in the description of perception and actual production of speech.[1] They can also be used in simulation experiments performed, for example, by means of electronic computers.

---

[1] Both problems are extremely complex and poorly understood. They involve many mechanisms other than grammar and make use of nonlinguistic situations. Even simpler studies, such as building a syntactic analyzer, constitute a difficult subject of research. Very few such analyzers have been built so far [A. K. Joshi, *Transformational Analysis by Computer*, U.S. Dept. H.E.W., 1968; S. Petrick, "A Recognition for Transformational Grammars," Ph.D. Thesis, M.I.T., 1965; J. Friedman, *A Computer Model for Transformational Grammar* (New York: American Elsevier Publishing Company, 1971)].

The problem of recognizing sentences suggests a new condition that should be imposed on grammars for natural languages. A sentence analyzer is a device that, given the grammar of a language and a string on the terminal alphabet of the language, will indicate among other things whether or not the string belongs to the language. Since the listener can always tell whether or not a string is in his language, natural languages are not only recursively enumerable, but they are also recursive.

The recognition and production of speech provide another argument for the framework that we present here. The processes we are interested in are entirely mechanical. The placement of the article to the left of a noun, the placement of suffixes, and their changes at the end of nouns and of verbs are entirely mechanical processes, never requiring conscious activity. This is one reason why we consider mechanical devices such as Turing machines and rewriting systems for the description of natural languages. We will use other properties of natural languages to restrict the class (we will also say the power) of their possible grammars.

Historically, much valuable work has been done by linguists who used tools that were as restricted (weak) as possible. The power of the tools (i.e., of the formal apparatus) was increased only when new facts were encountered that the weaker tools could not handle.

With whatever natural language it has been tried, the study of certain abstract devices involving special families of strings has proved extremely fruitful.

5.3

Linguistic Motivation

We shall now see why and how the concepts presented in earlier chapters are put to use in linguistics.

5.3.1
LINGUISTIC FACTS

We have mentioned how natural languages are described by structural linguists: Given the English alphabet V, the set of all strings V^* that can be built on the alphabet contains the English language; or else, given the lexicon W of all English words or morphemes, W^* contains English as a subset. The problem for the linguist is to provide statements (rules) that will separate the strings that correspond to English sentences or discourses from other strings that are considered ungrammatical by native speakers of English.[2] In order to arrive at such rules, one must study individual strings that occur in natural languages.

---

[2] What is being said of English is, of course, true of any natural language.

Let us consider, for example, the constraints that hold between subjects and verbs in English. The sequence of the two words *John* (subject) and *drinks* (verb)

John drinks

is an English sentence, but the sequence

drinks John

is not. The word *drinks* is only one of the forms of the verb. We easily verify that the string

John drank

is a sentence but that the string

drank John

is not. But if we replace *drinks* (or *drank*) by *drink*, then we notice that neither

(a) *John drink*   nor   (b) *drink John*

is an English sentence. We account for the impossibility of string (b) by means of the constraint on the word order between subjects and verbs. But in string (a), the order is respected, though the string is not English. We then have to introduce a new constraint stating that for certain subjects, verbs take certain endings. This rule is confirmed by pairs of strings such as

 Boys drink
*Boys drinks

which exhibit a different type of agreement, since in the preceding sentences we had

*John drink
John drinks.

There are other constraints between subjects and verbs, independently of the fact that not every subject goes with every verb ENDING. It is easy to observe that not every subject is semantically compatible with every VERB. The following sequences are not English sentences:[3]

---

[3] We have not defined the notions "subject" and "verb" but are using them as in traditional grammar. In fact, the only correct way of defining these concepts uses the constraints we have observed here.

*Vases dream
*Authorship dreams

(i.e., the verb *to dream* has, in general, only human subjects).

We can represent certain constraints by drawing an arch between the constrained items of the sentence:[4]

John drinks.

In fact, we are faced in the preceding examples with constraints between subject (a noun) and verb, namely lexical items, and also between lexical items and endings, which are usually called grammatical items (here, the *s* of *boys*, the *s* of *dreams*), and we should have patterns such as

John drinks

where the upper arch is intended to represent the constraint between lexical items and the lower one corresponds to the relation between the subject and the ending -*s* of the verb. Such constraints can be studied, and some of their formal properties abstracted from further empirical data.

Sentences such as

John often drinks

John, when he is tired, drinks

John, when he has finished the work that Paul gives him, drinks

show that the constraints we observed may operate even when subjects and verbs are separated by strings of arbitrary length. Moreover, within a constraint (i.e., under one such arch) the same constraint may again hold.

These examples are drawn from syntax, but we could as well talk about phonological constraints. If we study the ending -*s* (for verbs or for nouns), we notice that it is pronounced differently ($/z/$ or $/s/$)[5] according to the nature of the phoneme that precedes it: Compare *seeds* and *seats*, *robes*, and *ropes*, and so on. In other words, a constraint holds between the *s* and the phoneme that precedes it. We shall say that the subject-verb constraint is infinite, since it can operate between terms separated by an arbitrarily large number

---

[4] Underlying this representation is the fact that constraints operate between two items only. If there existed constraints holding among, say, three items, we would have to use some other device. It is an empirical fact that most (if not all) constraints can be reduced, in some sense, to binary ones.

[5] Phonemes (i.e., sounds) will be written between slashes in order to distinguish them from letters.

of words. On the other hand, the phonological constraint is finite. The distance counted in number of phonemes occurring between the constrained phonemes is finite (zero in our example).

These are some of the formal properties that we will study more closely. However, constraints are not limited to such simple types. Constraints exist also between strings. The shapes of the constrained strings can be extraordinarily varied, which makes it important to devise special methods for describing these phenomena. Not all constraints can be observed as easily as in the previous examples, where there is unanimous agreement as to which strings are in the English language and which are not. In numerous examples it is very hard to judge unequivocally. Judgments of grammaticality may differ among people, or even for the same person at different times. To state a safe observation in linguistics is equivalent to performing a good experiment in physics. It has to be replicable under the same given conditions by any specialist in the discipline.

There are also constraints whose nature is far from being clear. We find, for example, that the sentence

The boy was sleeping, and John was able to work

is quite normal, but we feel quite clearly that the "sentence"

The boy was sleeping, and this ball is an ellipsoid

is anomalous, although it is syntactically parallel to the preceding one. Some kind of constraint between the two strings occurring on each side of *and* has been violated, but its nature is hard to describe. In the first sentence, we perceive a relation between the two members of the conjunction: The fact that the boy was sleeping allowed John to work, presumably because the place was more quiet or because John did not have to watch or take care of the boy. No relation of this kind is perceived in the second example. Perhaps we have here the source of the difficulty, but the relation depends very much on the particular pair of sentences in the conjunction, and in fact depends on the interpretation of the sentences in terms of everyday life. In such a situation, it is impossible to think of what could be the elements of a description of the correct sentences. At any rate, they are in large part nonlinguistic, and the only thing we can point out is that the two members of a conjunction should be constrained in terms of some parallelism or similarity.

The preceding observation is hardly a linguistic fact. Other phenomena involving meaning might be approached in a more systematic way. We have already given examples of relations between lexical items (between subject and verb). Such relations are more general. For example, there is a relation between the verb and its object in the sentence

John is writing a book.

The objects of *to write* have to correspond to things from everyday life (or from some science) that are writable, and a string such as

John is writing an alligator

cannot be interpreted as a sentence, under the common meaning of *alligator* (animal of a certain type).

To succeed in describing a language as a subset of the free monoid generated by its lexicon would already be quite an achievement. So far, linguists have not built any characteristic device of the Turing-machine type (with presumably several hundred thousand instructions) or any formal system that would only tell which strings built by means of the morphemes of a given natural language are grammatical and which are not. These devices could be such that no particular attention would be paid to the shape, number, or role of the rules, the only requirement being that they provide the characteristic distinction for each string (i.e., does or does not belong to the language). But linguists have much more ambition for the grammars they construct. It is not sufficient to provide rules that state only, for example, that the string

(1) *John works at night*

is a sentence of English, while the string

(2) *John work at night*

is not. The rules must also show why this is so. The reason for excluding (2) from English (number agreement between subject and verb) is different from the reason for excluding (3) (word order):

(3) *Works John night at.*

If one were using only a characteristic device, (2) and (3) would be assigned "zeros," and (1) a "one," or (2) and (3) would not be generated at all, but no difference would ever be stated between (2) and (3). From both the descriptive and explanatory points of view this situation is quite inadequate.

The description of sentences involves many constraints. We will require that a grammar explicitly describe these constraints, thus pinpointing the reasons why strings are grammatical or not—that is, why they do or do not constitute a human language.

Constraints by no means occur randomly, even if in certain cases they fluctuate from speaker to speaker in some imprecise way. Mathematical linguistics, as we understand it here, can help classify constraints according to some of their formal features—the features that are independent of the meaning of the items involved. For a constraint to operate on elementary items (morphemes, phonemes) or on strings, or to be finite or infinite, are among such formal features. Mathematical linguistics can provide precise definitions and abstract characterizations of various families of strings, and of constraints.

5.3.2
THE USE OF SYMBOLS

Statements in traditional grammars are loose and imprecise. Rules often have as many exceptions as successful applications. One reason is that most of the grammatical terms that appear in rules never receive any substantial definition. These terms are used in various contexts; they often undergo slight modifications (by means of adjective adjunction, for example) according to circumstances; then their meaning shifts, and it can be corrected only by the user's intuition, always in an unclear way. Also, quite often, a certain term is given different names for the sole purpose of improving the style of the statement in which it appears.

Such a state of affairs can be remedied by giving to terms precise and operational definitions, which is an empirical question. At the same time a symbol (a name) is attached to each term. Usually a symbol may not have qualifiers such as adjectives adjoined to it, unless a precise procedure is given that will state all changes. From the point of view of reproducing concepts consistently, the use of symbols will avoid many difficulties.

5.3.3
TERMINAL AND AUXILIARY
VOCABULARIES

In § 3.1.3 we gave certain examples of auxiliary and terminal symbols. We consider here some of their uses. Sentences, as they are observed in texts or conversations, will be described as sequences of elementary units: phonemes, morphemes and words. These sets of elements will play the role of what we called terminal vocabularies.

Many difficult problems arise in the attempt to factor a sentence into phonemes or into words. A typical question that recurs constantly is the following. We mentioned that the ending -s in *seeds* and *seats* was not pronounced in the same way. But we know that these two phonemes correspond to a single grammatical process, and moreover we can predict, by looking at the phoneme that precedes it, how the corresponding letter *s* will be pronounced. The question then is: Do we have two different units /s/ and /z/, or a single unit modified by the environment? Notice that the question does not arise in all contexts. The words *mace* and *maze* end in /s/ and /z/, respectively, but these phonemes do not correspond to any grammatical process, and the string /ma/ to which they might appear to be appended does not have any independent occurrence as *seed* and *seat* do.[6] In this case the solution is to have two units /s/ and /z/ occurring in *mace* and *maze*, whereas the suffix *-s* corresponds to one unit that may be realized as /s/ or /z/ according to its left context.

It is quite clear that /s/ and /z/ belong to the terminal alphabet of English, but the status of the ending *-s* has not been defined. We could arbitrarily agree that the ending is always the terminal phoneme /s/ and that it can be modified, but we could just as well consider the letter *s* as an auxiliary symbol (i.e., member of V_A) to which terminal rules apply, providing the corresponding phonemes. This auxiliary symbol would be neutral with respect to /s/ and /z/ and would have a status very close to what is called an archiphoneme.

In § 1.3.1 we mentioned a building process for families of strings such as

John is strong and stupid,
John is tall, strong, and stupid,
John is fat, . . . , tall, strong, and stupid

Starting with a string of the form

(1) *John is X and stupid*

(where X is a variable holding for a sequence of at least one adjective), we build the other strings by inserting an adjective to the right of *is*. But we have in English other families of sentences that are closely related to the preceding ones—for example,

John (was + becomes + became + stays + stayed + · · ·) X and stupid

[where X is the same variable as in (1) above]. The building process here is quite similar. We have to insert an adjective to the right of *was*, or of *becomes*, or of *stays*, or of *stayed*, and so on. We then need as many rules as there are verbs that can occupy the position of *is* in (1). A natural way to state the similarity between these verbs is to give them a common name—for example,

---

[6] This property of individual or autonomous occurrence should not be considered as a general test for obtaining individual morphemes. There are cases in English where it does not apply, and in many languages stem morphemes cannot stand as independent words.

Vcop (for copula verb). We will then have a single general rule: Insert an adjective to the right of *Vcop* in the sequence

(2) *John Vcop X and stupid*

Vcop is a symbol that never appears in the English terminal language. *Vcop* will be an element of the auxiliary alphabet (or vocabulary) V_A needed for the description of English.

Notice that we already have been using more or less explicitly other auxiliary symbols. We repeatedly used the term adjective to refer to terminal words such as *tall, strong, . . . , stupid*—in fact, we have been giving the common name "adjective" (we will write *Adj*) to these items. We can now write (2) more conveniently in the following way:

(2') *John Vcop Adj (Adj)* and Adj*

where the adjunctions occur immediately to the right of *Vcop*.

In § 5.3.1 we used the terms "noun" and "verb," which are in fact names given to whole classes of English words. We will now refer to them as *N* and *V*, respectively. These two symbols are also members of the auxiliary vocabulary V_A. In fact, syntax often deals with classes such as *Adj, N, V* rather than with individual morphemes. Thus, if V_T is the set of the morphemes of English, syntax rather deals with some sort of morphic image[7] of V_T^* into $(V_A \cup V_T)^*$, namely with strings such as *N Vcop Adj* and Adj*, which is a member of $(V_A \cup V_T)^*$. The definitions we gave in Chapter III for rewriting systems will apply exactly for the description of natural languages. Their grammars will be considered as sets of rewriting rules.

Our previous insertion rule can be formulated in the following way:

> *N Vcop Adj (Adj)* and Adj*
> $\longrightarrow$ *N Vcop Adj Adj (Adj)* and Adj*

and we have *N, Vcop, Adj* $\in V_A$, *and* $\in V_T$. For natural languages the problem has two facets. First we need to determine V_T and V_A, and second we have to

---

[7] The syntactic classes are not equivalence classes; since we have, for example, $\{Vcop\} \nsubseteq V$, the image of V_T^* cannot be a morphic image. Various morphisms are involved, but in a quite complicated way. For example, the verbs called *Vcop* were equivalent with respect to the adjectives occurring to their right. If, instead, we choose the expression *on his feet*, we notice that

John (is + was + stays + stayed) on his feet

is a sentence, but not

John (becomes + became) on his feet

factor the strings—that is, to state the rewriting rules. These two processes depend on one another: In order to factor a string, one needs a reference vocabulary, and in order to define reference vocabularies, one has to factor strings. However, building a grammar is not a circular procedure, but a series of successive approximations, each step of which consists in making assumptions about parts of the grammar, and then in deriving conclusions about other parts of the grammar.

5.4

_____

Grammar Rules

We have given an example of a grammatical statement that describes certain conjunctions of adjectives. The point is that we can replace naturally a statement made in the English language by a rule of a rewriting system. Many questions can be raised about this rule. Why is it not formulated as

>   *N Vcop (Adj)* Adj and Adj*
> $\longrightarrow$ *N Vcop (Adj)* Adj Adj and Adj*

which would correspond to the insertion of *Adj* to the left of *and*? Or else why not describe such sequences as resulting from the merging of several sentences? The sentence

John is tall, strong, and stupid

would be the result of the merging of a pair of sentences such as

John is tall

and

John is strong and stupid

which could be described more generally by the rule

>   *N Vcop Adj and N is Adj (Adj)* and Adj*
> $\longrightarrow$ *N Vcop Adj Adj (Adj)* and Adj.*

But those are all empirical questions that can be solved only by linguistic analysis. In any case, it remains true that the rule can be formulated as a rewriting rule [i.e., each side of the arrow is an element of $(V_A \cup V_T)^*$, and the arrow is to be interpreted as in § 3.1].

The axiom of the grammar of a natural language will always be S, for sentence. The axiom S will be left undefined, its empirical interpretation being left to the intuition of the speaker. This situation is quite normal, since the final aim of a grammar is the description of all sentences, and since the agreement among speakers about what is and what is not a sentence is fairly good. The main purpose of using formalized rules is to avoid the imprecision of natural languages in syntactic statements. In the nonformalized version of the rule for conjunction, for example, we use the word "insert"; we could just as well use the words "place," "add," "introduce," and so on. Such words often have connotations that are irrelevant to the construction being described. We eliminate these superfluous meanings by using formalized rules. Also, formalized rules allow a much greater generality. For example, we could describe the change in the ending s by the rule

$$fP \# s \rightarrow fP \# /z/$$

for certain P's (where fP is the root, P is its rightmost phoneme, and the root is separated from the ending s by the marker $\#$). This rule, although different from the conjunction rule, is still a rule of a rewriting system.

In a large number of cases, by using the simple apparatus of rewriting systems, we are able to state rules that correspond to linguistic phenomena as different as syntax and phonology. Such a unified way of describing linguistic facts implies something about the nature of linguistic behavior.

5.5

Rules and Computing Devices

When we compare the ways Turing machines and rewriting systems perform computations, we find important differences in the corresponding statements. There is a sense in which the degree of formalization of the computations that automata realize is too high, when it comes to describing natural languages.

5.5.1
DELETIONS

Consider, for example, the problem of deleting, by means of an automaton, the substring ba of the tape

(1)

$\#$	a	b	b	b	b	a	a	a	$\#$

The result is the tape

(2)

#	a	b	b	b	#	#	a	a	#

with two blanks # occurring between $a\,b\,b\,b$ and $a\,a$. For various applications, the interesting result is the string $a\,b^3\,a^2$—that is, the tape

(3)

#	a	b	b	b	a	a	#

But in order to obtain (3), we have to apply to (2) a certain number of operations: Either move $a\,a$ two squares to the left, or else move $a\,b\,b\,b$ two squares to the right, or else move $a\,a$ one square to the left and $a\,b\,b\,b$ one square to the right.[8]

In cases where we are interested only in the zeroing procedure, rewriting rules such as

$$b\,a \to e \quad \text{or} \quad a\,b^4\,a^3 \to a\,b^3\,a^2 \quad \text{and so on}$$

are much preferable. However, zeroing a substring of a string and replacing it by blanks could receive some linguistic interpretation. One could, for example, link blanks to the pauses that occur between certain phrases. Consider the positions of the commas in the sentences

to John, I gave a book, to Paul, a knife,
John, when he is hungry, eats a lot.

We could try to relate the corresponding pauses to deleted substrings. It is rather natural to relate the pause between *Paul* and *a knife* to a sequence of blanks resulting from the deletion of *I gave*, but it is much harder to do so for the other pauses above; they seem to be related to permutations rather than to deletions. Moreover, in many instances no pause appears in the position of the deleted material. In the sentence

I gave John a book and a knife

no pause is allowed between *and* and the following *a*, although this sentence presumably results from the deletion of *I gave him* in the corresponding

---

[8] When we defined the language of a Turing machine as the set of strings that resulted from a finite computation, we were ambiguous about the nature of the result. We considered it both as a tape with possible blanks occurring between letters and as a string where no blanks may appear. The notions are equivalent when, by convention, # is equal to e, or when special instructions shift the substrings in order to erase all #'s.

position of the sentence:

I gave John a book and I gave him a knife.

Even in the favorable cases where blanks and pauses could be linked together, the number of blanks, which is variable, ought to correspond to
pauses of variable importance; but, as Z. S. Harris noted,[9] no phenomenon
of this type has ever been observed in any natural language.

5.5.2
INSERTIONS

Insertion of a string into some other string is a device frequently used in
linguistic descriptions. Its formalization raises questions that are similar to
some of the preceding ones.

Consider the sentence

He sleeps

and the insertion of the adverb *often* between subject and verb, or, more
generally, between N and V on the tape

$$(1) \quad \boxed{\# \mid N \mid V \mid \#}$$

the result being the tape

$$(2) \quad \boxed{\# \mid N \mid often \mid V \mid \#}$$

In (1) we have to either shift N one square to the left or V one square to the
right, in order to provide a blank square for *often*. There is no linguistic
motivation for choosing between these two solutions. Even worse, this
choice appears to have no linguistic relevance at all. The problem arises only
because we are using an automaton to describe the phenomenon, and this
model imposes too much structure on the sequences of words. Again, it is
preferable to use the rewriting rule

$N\ V \rightarrow N\ often\ V$

since it reflects more adequately the observed building process.

---

[9] In *Mathematical Structure of Language* (New York: John Wiley & Sons, Inc.,
1968).

5.5.3
PERMUTATIONS

There are sentences that can be paired together, and that differ only by an inversion of two of their terms. We have, for example, pairs such as

John will go there
Will John go there?

The natural way to relate such sentences is by assuming a "question transformation," which is a rule that can be written

$$NP \; Aux \; V \; X$$
$$\rightarrow Aux \; NP \; V \; X.$$

Here *NP* corresponds to subjects, *Aux* to auxiliaries such as *will, could, . . . , V* is the main verb, and the variable *X* ranges over the remainder of the sentences. What is important for the description to retain is the relative positions of the subject *NP* and the auxiliary *Aux*. It makes no sense to ask whether the transformation moved *NP* to the right of *Aux* or *Aux* to the left of *NP*. Using a Turing machine forces us to choose between one of the two building processes, while the rewriting rule simulates the process as it is understood on syntactic grounds.

VI

Finite-State Processes

The finite-state type of building process can be
described in various ways. The languages of these
ways of description have been called finite-state
languages, regular languages, or regular events.
We will call them Kleene's languages
(or K-languages) after the logician who first
characterized them mathematically.[1]

6.1

Finite Automaton

A finite automaton is an abstract machine that, like a Turing machine, has a
central unit with a finite number of states. The set of states will be denoted as

$$\Sigma = \{S_i : 0 \leqslant i \leqslant n\}.$$

Among these states, we distinguish S_0 as the initial state, and a subset
Σ_f of Σ as final states. The letters of an input alphabet $V = \{a_j : 1 \leqslant j \leqslant m\}$
are written on the squares of an input tape.

The major restriction on Turing machines is that the head can only
read symbols on the tape; it can neither write nor modify any input letter.

---

[1] S. C. Kleene, "Representation of Events in Nerve Nets and Finite Automata,"
in *Automata Studies* (Princeton, N.J.: Princeton University Press, 1951).

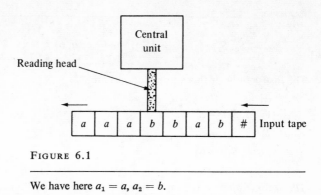

FIGURE 6.1

We have here $a_1 = a$, $a_2 = b$.

A less significant restriction[2] limits the movements of the tape to one direction (e.g., right-to-left). Given the conventions adopted for Turing machines (§ 2.1.2), the instructions that direct the computations will all be of a single type:

$$(a_i, S_j) \to (L, S_k).$$

In state S_j, reading the symbol a_i, the automaton switches to state S_k and moves the tape one square to the left. Since the symbol L will appear in all instructions, we can omit it altogether. We now write all instructions in the form

$$(a_i, S_j) \to S_k,$$

with the same interpretation as before.

All computations start in state S_0, with the reading head on the leftmost square of the input tape. The instructions determine the course of the computation. If a computation of an input string f ends in a final state (i.e., $\in \Sigma_f$) reading the symbol $\#$ to the right of f, f is said to be "accepted" by the automaton. The set of all f's accepted by a given automaton constitutes its language.

The blank symbol $\#$ does not play any important role here. With finite automata, the amount of tape used is always limited to the input tape; excess blank tape cannot be supplied as for Turing machines. The symbol $\#$ thus is a simple punctuation mark that could be dispensed with by modifying the definition of a computation.

[2] It can be proven that allowing both movements does not change the class of characterized languages [M. O. Rabin and D. Scott, "Finite Automata and Their Decision Problems," *I.B.M. J. Res. Develop.*, vol. 3 (1959).

EXAMPLE

$$\Sigma = \{S_0, S_1\}, \qquad \Sigma_f = \{S_1\}, \qquad V = \{a, b\}.$$

The instructions of this automaton (A) are:

(1) $(a, S_0) \rightarrow S_0$

(2) $(b, S_0) \rightarrow S_1$

(3) $(b, S_1) \rightarrow S_1$.

The computation of the input string a^3b^2 is shown in Figure 6.2. In state S_0, the automaton can read any number of a's. When the first b appears under the reading

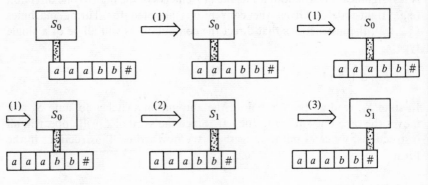

FIGURE 6.2

head, the automaton switches from S_0 to state S_1, where it can read any number of b's. When the blank symbol $\#$ appears under the head, the automaton blocks in the final state S_1. The corresponding accepted strings have the shape a^*bb^*. Alternatively, in state S_0, the automaton could start reading b's directly. This corresponds to the set of accepted strings $bb^* \subset a^*bb^*$. Once in state S_1 (i.e., after it has read at least one b), if an a appears under the reading head, the automaton blocks; the input string is not in the language. It is then clear that the language accepted by automaton (A) is the set a^*bb^*.

6.2

Other Interpretations

We will now give interpretations of these sets of triples other than that of a machine accepting, or recognizing, strings.

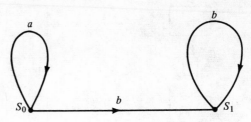

FIGURE 6.3

6.2.1
FINITE-STATE GRAPHS

We can interpret a triple (or an instruction) in the following way: The nodes of a directed graph, called a state graph, correspond to the states of the machine. An edge is constructed between two nodes S_i and S_k in this order, if S_i and S_k belong to an instruction $(a_i, S_j) \rightarrow S_k$; this edge is then labeled a_i.

The set of instructions of our example (A) can be represented by the state graph in Figure 6.3.

The relation between the graph and the language of an automaton is easily obtained when we consider the graph as a language-producing device. Starting in initial state S_0, we travel inside the graph, ending in one of the final states of Σ_f. If we display from left to right the edge labels encountered during each move, we have a word. The set of all words obtainable in this way is the language of the automaton.

In our example we start in S_0 and end in S_1. The circuits all differ by the numbers of times (including zero) that the two loops a and b are used. If we move three times in loop a, then move to S_1, and then move four times in loop b, we obtain the word *aaabbbb*.

6.2.2
PRODUCING AUTOMATON

When we defined the finite automaton in § 6.1, we interpreted the instructions as if they constituted a recognition procedure. With the same central unit, but with a writing head, and starting with an empty tape (i.e., filled with blanks) in state S_0, we can read the instructions

$$(a_i, S_j) \rightarrow S_k$$

in the following way. In state S_j, the automaton writes a_i on a blank square and moves the tape one square to the left. If a computation stops in a state of Σ_f, then the content of the tape is a word in the language of the automaton.

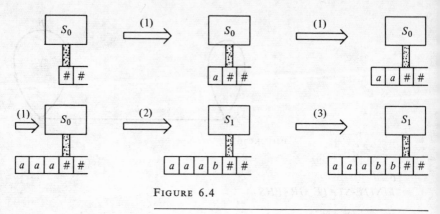

FIGURE 6.4

The sequence of instructions is exactly the same as in Figure 6.2.

The word *aaabb* of our previous example will be generated as shown in Figure 6.4.

6.2.3
FINITE-STATE GRAMMARS

We can also interpret the instructions as rewriting rules. The set of states Σ will be the auxiliary alphabet V_A, while V, the alphabet of the automaton, will be V_T. The initial state S_0 will be the axiom.

With each instruction

$$(a_i, S_j) \rightarrow S_{k'}.$$

we associate the rewriting rule

$$S_j \rightarrow a_i S_{k'}.$$

Moreover, for all states $S_l \in \Sigma_f$, we add the terminal rule

$$S_l \rightarrow e.$$

All derivations start with S_0. Each step is of the form

$$\rightarrow g\, S_j \qquad \text{where} \qquad g \in V_T^*.$$

When the rule $S_j \rightarrow a_i S_k$ applies, we obtain the next step: $g\, a_i\, S_k$. The application of a rule reproduces exactly a move in the corresponding edge of the state graph.[3]

If a step of a derivation is of the form

$$\rightarrow f S_i \quad \text{where } S_i \in \Sigma_f,$$

the rule $S_i \rightarrow e$ may apply, which yields f as a member of the language generated by the grammar.

EXAMPLE _____

The automaton (A) has for instructions

$$(a, S_0) \rightarrow S_0$$
$$(b, S_0) \rightarrow S_1$$
$$(b, S_1) \rightarrow S_1.$$

Applying to it the procedure just given provides the rules

(1) $S_0 \rightarrow aS_0$
(2) $S_0 \rightarrow bS_1$
(3) $S_1 \rightarrow bS_1$

respectively. The terminal rule

(4) $S_1 \rightarrow e$

corresponds to the final state S_1.

The derivation of the word *aaabb* is

$S_0 \rightarrow aS_0$	by rule (1)
$\rightarrow aaS_0$	by rule (1)
$\rightarrow aaaS_0$	by rule (1)
$\rightarrow aaabS_1$	by rule (2)
$\rightarrow aaabbS_1$	by rule (3)
$\rightarrow aaabb$	by rule (4).

6.2.4
A LANGUAGE THAT IS NOT
A K-LANGUAGE

K-languages have restricted shapes. An example of a language that is not a K-language is the language $L = \{a^n b^n : n > 0\}$. We indicate why it

---

[3] The procedure that associates the rules of a rewriting system with the instructions of the automaton is very similar to the one we used to show equivalence between Turing machines and formal systems (§ 4.3).

cannot be generated by any K-grammar. Consider a step in the derivation of the string $a^m b^m$ that has the form

$$\rightarrow a^m b^p A \qquad p < m.$$

Notice that such a step must occur, since only a finite number of terminal symbols are generated by each application of a rule. Since m may be arbitrarily large with respect to p, there must exist in any K-grammar generating L an auxiliary symbol G, which is the first step in derivations of the form

$$G \rightarrow \cdots \rightarrow b^k G \rightarrow \cdots \rightarrow b^{2k} G \rightarrow \cdots \rightarrow b^{ik} G \rightarrow \cdots \rightarrow \cdots$$

This means that in the corresponding state graph there is a loop that starts from G and arrives at G. The index i counts the number of passages in the loop. There must also exist at the same time a derivation of the type

$$G \rightarrow \cdots \rightarrow b^l$$

if G is to become terminal. Under such conditions, from the step

$$\rightarrow a^m b^p G$$

it is possible to generate the infinite family of strings

$$\{a^m b^{p+ik+l} : 0 \leqslant i\}.$$

At most one of them belongs to L. Thus, the language L cannot be a K-language.

6.2.5
REMARKS ON INTERPRETATION

It is quite clear that all the interpretations we have given are equivalent. If we are given one of the devices that we considered, we can interpret it in terms of any of the others without affecting the language associated with the device. In fact, these mechanisms are all redundant. We again have an example in which using a certain apparatus does not contribute in any way to the structure of the described family of strings. Indeed, the structure is entirely captured by the single notion of the algebraic mapping between $\Sigma \times V$ and Σ as discussed in § 6.4 and needs no extra hardware such as a central unit, reading or writing head, graph, and so on. Although such devices can aid our intuitive understanding of some of the properties of the K-language, in general we can reach deep properties only by applying abstract algebraic methods to the study of the mapping, ignoring the "concrete" aspect of the defining mechanisms.

Further, from an empirical point of view, the use of the terms acceptance, generation, production, and so on may confuse many linguists and blur the abstract character of the definition of natural language that we are now investigating. In fact none of the described devices is capable of recognizing or generating strings by itself. Such devices merely characterize a certain family of strings from an abstract point of view. This abstract point of view now prevails among linguists, who see one of the major problems of linguistics to be the characterizing of natural languages in such a way that the production and perception of speech (although these are important and difficult problems) are immaterial to the study of language structure.

6.3

Regular Expressions

The expressions we have been using, such as $V\{a, b\}^*$ (i.e., concatenation of two sets, star set), can be used to describe all K-languages.

Let V be an alphabet. We will define on it by recursion the family of regular sets:

RULE (i) $X \subset V$; any such finite set X is a regular set.

RULE (ii)   If X_1 and X_2 are regular sets, the concatenation $X_1 X_2$ is a regular set.

RULE (iii)   If $X_1, X_2, \ldots, X_n$ are regular sets, then the set $\{X_1, X_2, \ldots, X_n\}^*$ is regular.

All regular sets are built by application of these three rules. An expression defined in terms of these notations corresponds to each regular set.

The sense of this construction is the following:

RULE (i)   trivially provides regular sets (i.e., finite sets).

RULE (ii)   defines the product of two sets, and thus of any finite number of sets. This provides words in V.

RULE (iii)   allows definition of infinite sets, building from finite ones, by performing all possible products of the X_i's in any order, and with any number of repetitions.

Regular set is another name for K-language, as we can see by generalizing the procedure of the following example, in which a state graph is assigned a regular expression.

$$V = \{a, b, c\}$$

The regular expression is

$$L = c\{a^*ba^*, b\{a, b, c\}^*a, c^*\}^*c.$$

To a product X_1X_2 we assign the labeled type of graph in Figure 6.5.[4]

$$X_1 \qquad\qquad X_2$$

FIGURE 6.5

To each star operating on n expressions $X_1, X_2, \ldots, X_n$ we assign the labeled type of graph in Figure 6.6.

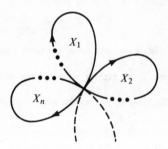

FIGURE 6.6

We will use the fact that if R is a regular expression, then eR, Re, eRe, and so on are also regular expressions with the edges of their graphs labeled e. Using this convention, we now write L as

$$L = c\{ea^*ba^*e, b\{a, b, c\}^*a\, ec^*e\}^*c,$$

and assign to it the graph of Figure 6.7, in which the initial node (I) and the final node (F) are distinguished. This state graph generates the language L.

---

[4] Edges interrupted by dots generally mean there are complex graphs, not simple edges, in the corresponding positions. When each of the symbols $X_1, X_2, \ldots, X_n$ corresponds to a single letter, the dots can be replaced by a plain line.

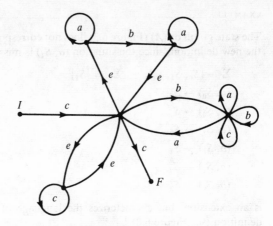

FIGURE 6.7

The three connected subgraphs attached to the central node correspond to the three expressions in the braces. We could have used other representations, such as one suppressing the two lower edges *e* and attaching the loop *c* directly to the central node.

Any K-language can be represented by a finite number of regular expressions.

*6.4

Algebraic System
Associated to a Finite Automaton

We now consider an algebraic system based on Schützenberger's definition of finite automaton. It uses the idea that an instruction $(a_i, S_j) \to S_k$ can be considered as a mapping between the cartesian product $\Sigma \times V$ and the set of the subsets of Σ: $\mathcal{F}(\Sigma)$.

6.4.1
AUTOMATA AND MAPPINGS

We modify the definition in § 6.1, retaining $V, \Sigma, S_0 \in \Sigma, \Sigma_f \in \Sigma$, and a set of instructions

$$(a_i, S_j) \to S_k$$

but requiring this set of instructions to be such that all possible situations [i.e., all pairs (a_i, S_j)] are present once and only once. In terms of a state graph, if V has m elements, from each node there are m edges leaving, each labeled by a different letter of V.

The state graph or (A) (Figure 6.3) does not correspond to a finite automaton under the new definition, since the situation (a, S_1) is missing. But the automaton

$$\Sigma = \{S_0, S_1, S_2\}, \qquad \Sigma_f = \{S_1\}$$
$$(a, S_0) \rightarrow S_0$$
$$(b, S_0) \rightarrow S_1$$
$$(a, S_1) \rightarrow S_2$$
$$(b, S_1) \rightarrow S_1$$
$$(a, S_2) \rightarrow S_2$$
$$(b, S_2) \rightarrow S_2$$

is an extension that characterizes the language of (A) and exemplifies the new definition (see Figure 6.8).

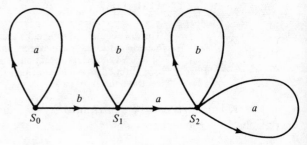

FIGURE 6.8

S_0 is the initial state and S_1 the final state. By adding new states to fulfill the condition, we changed Figure 6.3 to Figure 6.8. This procedure is quite general. Any automaton of the type of § 6.1 can be given the new form.

For each letter a_i, and for each state S_j, there is a certain state S_k such that $(S_j \rightarrow S_k)$ is the edge to which a_i is assigned. For a given a_i we can list all these edges (there are always $n = card\ (\Sigma)$ such edges). The instructions can thus be written in the following way:

$$\text{for } 1 \leqslant i \leqslant m: \qquad a_i \rightarrow \begin{pmatrix} S_0 \rightarrow S_{k_1} \\ S_1 \rightarrow S_{k_2} \\ \cdot \\ \cdot \\ \cdot \\ S_{n-1} \rightarrow S_{k_n} \end{pmatrix}$$

where the arrows indicate mappings.

Between the parentheses is a mapping of Σ into Σ, and one such mapping is associated with each letter of V. In other words, we have a correspondence between the elements of V and the mappings of Σ into Σ.

We now have: (i) the set V, on the elements of which we can define an associative product (i.e., concatenation), the resulting set being V^*, (ii) the set Σ^Σ of the applications of Σ into Σ, on which we can also define an associative product, since the product of two such applications is an application. The resulting set is Σ^Σ again.

We study next the relations between the two products.

In terms of automata, this study is quite natural. When an automaton reads (or writes) a string, switching from state to state, we see that it associates the concatenation of a string of letters to the products of the mappings of Σ^Σ that correspond to each letter. Consider, for example, an automaton that reads the string $a_{i_1} a_{i_2}$.

1. When it reads the letter a_{i_1}, it switches from S_j to S_k.
2. When it reads the letter a_{i_2}, it switches from S_k to S_l.
3. When it reads the string $a_{i_1} a_{i_2}$, it switches from S_j to S_l.

Let μ be the mapping between V^* and Σ^Σ. We write the elements of Σ^Σ in the following way:

$$
\begin{pmatrix}
S_{j_1} \to S_{k_1} \\
S_{j_2} \to S_{k_2} \\
\cdot \\
\cdot \\
\cdot \\
S_{j_n} \to S_{k_n}
\end{pmatrix}
$$

We then have the correspondence:

$$
\begin{pmatrix}
\cdot \\
\cdot \\
\cdot \\
a_{i_1} \xrightarrow{\ \mu\ } \quad S_j \to S_k \\
\cdot \\
\cdot \\
\cdot
\end{pmatrix}
$$

$$\begin{pmatrix} \vdots \\ a_{i_2} \xrightarrow{\ \mu\ } \ S_k \to S_l \\ \vdots \end{pmatrix}$$

$$\begin{pmatrix} \vdots \\ a_{i_1} a_{i_2} \xrightarrow{\ \mu\ } \ S_j \to S_l \\ \vdots \end{pmatrix}$$

More formally, let f be the mapping between V and Σ^Σ defined by the instructions of an automaton:

$$f: V \to \Sigma^\Sigma, \quad \text{then } f(S_j, a_i) = S_k;$$

$f(S_j, a_i) = S_k$ is defined for all situations (a_i, S_j) according to the revised definition of finite automaton. Since the mapping f was defined only for letters (a_i), we must extend its definition to strings on the a_i's. The extension of f, denoted f^*, is defined by induction:

(i) $f^*(S_i, e) = S_i$ for $0 \leqslant i \leqslant n$,

(ii) $f^*(S_i, ga_j) = f(f^*(S_i, g), a_j)$ for $0 \leqslant i < n; 1 \leqslant j \leqslant m; g \in V^*$.

Equations (i) associate e (the unit string of V^*) with the identity mapping of Σ^Σ.

Equations (ii) are read as follows. f^*, in the left member, associates a certain state S_r with a state S_i and a string ga_j, where $a_j \in V$. In the right member, f^* associates a certain S_t with S_i and with the string g. f (defined on the single letters only) associates S_r and the pair (S_t, a_j). In the right member f^* is defined on a string that is shorter by one than the string of the left member, which is the basis of the induction process.

6.4.2
THE MONOID OF AN AUTOMATON

As an example of the definition of f^*, let us compute f^* for the string a_1a_2.

$$f^*(S_i, a_1a_2) = f(f^*(S_i, a_1), a_2) \qquad \text{by (ii)},$$

$$f^*(S_i, a_1) = f(f^*(S_i, e), a_1) \qquad \text{by (ii)},$$

$$f^*(S_i, a_1) = f(S_i, a_1) \qquad \text{by (i)}.$$

We report the value obtained in the first equation, which yields

$$f^*(S_i, a_1a_2) = f(f(S_i, a_1), a_2)$$

for all S_i's and a_j's. Retranslating this equation in terms of μ, we have

$$\mu(a_1a_2) = \mu(a_1)\mu(a_2)$$

for all a_j's.

Thus, μ is a morphism (i.e., the two products in V^* and in Σ^Σ are compatible with the mapping μ), and we have the picture shown in Figure 6.9. The structure Σ^Σ is a finite monoid; μ is a mapping of the free monoid V^* into Σ^Σ. Then $\mu(V^*)$ is a finite submonoid of Σ^Σ. This finite submonoid is called the monoid associated with the automaton.

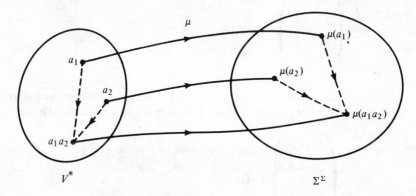

FIGURE 6.9

We study the monoid defined by the graph of Figure 6.10, or equivalently by the instructions:

$$(a, S_0) \to S_0; \quad (a, S_1) \to S_1; \quad (a, S_2) \to S_2; \quad (a, S_3) \to S_3;$$
$$(b, S_0) \to S_1; \quad (b, S_1) \to S_2; \quad (b, S_2) \to S_3; \quad (b, S_3) \to S_3.$$

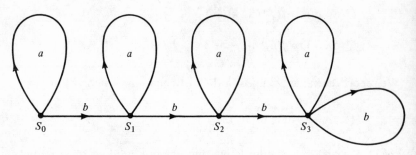

FIGURE 6.10

We define μ:

$$a \to \begin{pmatrix} S_0 \to S_0 \\ S_1 \to S_1 \\ S_2 \to S_2 \\ S_3 \to S_3 \end{pmatrix} = E, \text{ the identity mapping}$$

$$b \to \begin{pmatrix} S_0 \to S_1 \\ S_1 \to S_2 \\ S_2 \to S_3 \\ S_3 \to S_3 \end{pmatrix} = m$$

In order to obtain the other elements of $\mu(V^*)$, we have only to consider the powers of m, since the other products will not introduce any new elements. We thus have

$$m^2 = \begin{pmatrix} S_0 \to S_2 \\ S_1 \to S_3 \\ S_2 \to S_3 \\ S_3 \to S_3 \end{pmatrix} \leftarrow bb$$

$$m^3 = \begin{pmatrix} S_0 \rightarrow S_3 \\ S_1 \rightarrow S_3 \\ S_2 \rightarrow S_3 \\ S_3 \rightarrow S_3 \end{pmatrix} \leftarrow bbb$$

An element such as m^3 is called a zero, since any product containing m^3 will be equal to m^3. We are then sure that $\mu(V^*) = \{E, m, m^2, m^3\}$.

The table below lists the products of the finite monoid $\mu(V^*)$.

	E	m	m^2	m^3
E	E	m	m^2	m^3
m	m	m^2	m^3	m^3
m^2	m^2	m^3	m^3	m^3
m^3	m^3	m^3	m^3	m^3

In order to construct f^* (or μ), we used only the instructions of the automaton; we did not use S_0 or Σ_f. These elements are important for the definition of the language of the automaton.

We notice that a word g is accepted by an automaton if and only if

$$f^*(S_0, g) = S_p \in \Sigma_f.$$

—that is, if and only if μ maps g onto an application of Σ^Σ that maps the initial state onto a final state S_p.

In Figure 6.9 the set Σ^Σ contains a finite number of elements, and the infinite set V^* is divided into a corresponding finite set of equivalence classes. If we consider all the mappings of Σ^Σ that map S_0 onto S_p, $S_p \in \Sigma_f$, the union of the corresponding classes of V^* constitutes the language of the automaton. More generally, if μ is a morphism of a free monoid into a finite monoid, a K-language L is defined by the property

$$L = \mu^{-1}\mu(L).$$

The converse is also true: any set of strings L that has this property is a K-language.

$\mu\mu^{-1}(X)$ is the set Y of elements of V^* such that $\mu(Y) = X \subset \Sigma^\Sigma$.

Returning to our previous example (Figure 6.10), if we call S_0 the initial state, and S_3 the final state, the only element of Σ^Σ that maps S_0 to S_3 is m^3.

In V^*, the class of the string *bbb* corresponds to m^3. Since m^3 is a zero, multiplying it by any element leaves it unchanged. Correspondingly, adjoining any string to *bbb* leads to the elements of the class of *bbb*. In other words, the language of the automaton is the set of strings that contains at least three *b*'s.

6.5

Extensions of the Definition of Finite Automaton

Various extensions of the definitions of finite automata given in § 6.1 are often used. The extensions we shall now discuss do not change the power of the corresponding devices, since they still characterize K-language.

Of the possible extensions, one could consider using several initial states instead of one, using one final state instead of several, or requiring that S_0 be both the initial and the final state, and that a computation ends when the automaton returns to S_0 the first time. We have already considered allowing the tape to move back and forth, or to stop. The instructions would then have the form

$$(a_i, S_j) \to (M, S_k).$$

The movement M can be L (left), R (right), or N (none).

We can also allow instructions of the form

$$(e, S_j) \to S_k,$$

with the interpretation that the reading head does not read (i.e., reads e), that the tape does not move, and that the state S_j switches to S_k.

Though the edges of the state graphs were labeled with letters, we can label them with strings. We can also make special use of punctuation marks to the right (as we did with $\#$) or to the left of the input string.

None of these changes modifies the class of characterized languages.

A situation of special interest is one in which the automaton may have a set of instructions such that to a given situation there correspond several states. The automaton then has several instructions with the same left member, and it is called nondeterministic. For each nondeterministic finite automaton we can construct a deterministic one that generates the same language.

6.6

Formal Properties of K-languages.

K-languages constitute a family, denoted by $K(V)$, with remarkable properties. The family $K(V)$ is closed under the operations of union, intersection,
complementation, product, and star.

We suggest how some of these properties can be demonstrated by
giving corresponding constructions. In order to do so, we will use one of the
previously mentioned extensions, labeling the edges with the null string e.

6.6.1
UNION

Consider two K-languages defined by their state graphs. The two
initial nodes are I_1 and I_2; the two sets of final states are Σ_{f_1} and Σ_{f_2}.

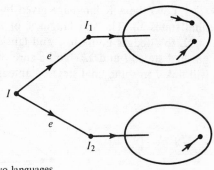

Union of two languages

FIGURE 6.11

The state graphs of the given languages are indicated with
circles. We have also indicated the initial states, and inside
the circles some final states.

We introduce a new node I, the initial node of the union language, and
connect the two graphs by drawing the edges II_1 and II_2 oriented from I to
I_1 and I_2, labeling both by the null string e (Figure 6.11). The language
defined by this graph, and which has the set $\Sigma_f = \Sigma_{f_1} \cup \Sigma_{f_2}$ for the set of
final states, is the union of the two given K-languages. Since it is defined by
a state graph, it is also a K-language (Figure 6.11).

6.6.2
PRODUCT

Given two K-languages L_1 (initial state I_1, final states Σ_{f_1}) and L_2 (initial state I_2, final states Σ_{f_2}) we obtain the product $L_1 L_2$ if we connect the two graphs with edges labeled e and going from each of the states Σ_{f_1} to I_2. The resulting state graph (initial state I_1, final states Σ_{f_2}) corresponds to the K-language $L_1 L_2$ (Figure 6.12).

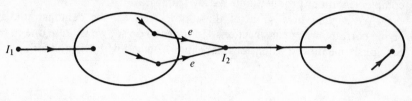

FIGURE 6.12

Product of two K-languages.

6.6.3
STAR

Let L be a K-language given by a state graph with initial state I and final states Σ_f. The star language of L is obtained by connecting the states of Σ_f to I (edges going to I and labeled e) and by keeping the same distinguished states I and Σ_f. To be sure of including e in the star language, we will link I to some final state by an edge labeled e (Figure 6.13).

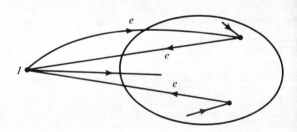

FIGURE 6.13

Star of a K-language.

6.7

Application to Syntax

We now illustrate how a state graph can be used in generating sentences, or equivalently, sequences of grammatical categories related to actual sentences by lexical substitutions.

The graph of Figure 6.14 generates strings of the form

subject—verb—direct object.

Subjects may be singular or plural. Singular subjects correspond to the path $(I, 1, 2)$, with the corresponding verb followed by the affix -s in present tense [path $(2, 10, 12)$]. Plural subjects may correspond to the following sequences:

1. Plural nouns: path $(I, 3, 4, 9)$.
2. Conjunction of singular and/or plural, nouns, with or without an expressed *and* separating them: paths $(I, 3, 4, 5, 6, 7, 8, 9)$. The paths $(4, 5)$ and $(8, 9)$ correspond to choice of singular (label E), or plural (label -s). The paths $(5, 6)$ correspond to the optional use of *and*. The loop $(4, 5, 6, 7, 8, 4)$ allows any number of conjoined nouns. In present plural, the verb V has no affix [edge $(11, 12)$ labeled E].

The types of direct objects we have allowed are identical with the types of subjects and are described by paths $(12, F)$.

Although the graph is complex, it does not describe a wide variety of structures. Noun phrases are only of the type *the N* (singular or plural). We must repeat identical descriptions. For example, if we include the description of relative clauses in the noun phrases we displayed, we have to add the corresponding graph to the nodes 2, 4, 8, and 14. For relative pronouns that are subjects, we must distinguish between singular and plural noun phrases, further complicating the graph. The duplications appearing on the graph cannot be avoided. (We distinguish singular subjects from plural ones because of the verb affix -s, though we do not have to make the distinction for objects.)

Such graphs are difficult to generalize, and additions often entail fundamental modifications. Look at Figure 6.14. If we want our description to include sentences with conjoined verbs, we need a loop with V in it. If we add the edges $(12, 2)$ labeled E and *and*, and similar edges between 12 and 9, the corresponding sentences may be of the type:

The boy purchased and drinks the wine.

But then ungrammatical mixtures of tenses are not prohibited. In the case of indefinite articles the situation is even more complicated. We can easily add an edge $(I, 1)$ labeled a (the indefinite article). We cannot do this between I and 3 because the graph would generate ungrammatical noun phrases such as *a boys* by path $(I, 3, 4, 9)$. In order to incorporate the article a, we must make fundamental changes in the graph.

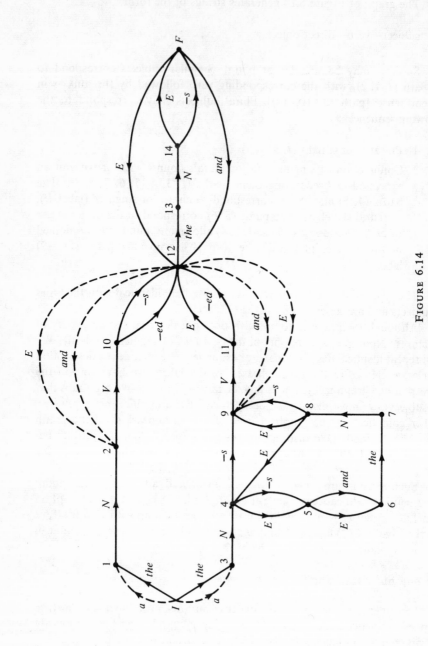

Mathematizin Adalticn Labortary

FIGURE 6.14

The dotted edges correspond to these additions

6.8

Application to Morphophonology

Finite-state devices have a certain adequacy for representing various finite constraints found within morphemes of natural languages. Markov's observations[5] on these bear on the distribution of vowels and consonants with respect to left contexts of finite length. Shannon[6] carried out a related study. For a given corpus, the frequency of occurrence of each letter of English (the space between words is considered as a letter) has been computed for each left context of k letters ($k = 0, 1, 2, \ldots, 5$). These frequencies can be used in building strings. At each step in the construction process, and in a left context of k letters, a new letter is randomly selected according to its frequency of occurrence. The result has a morphophonological pattern similar to English, and tends to resemble English more closely as k is increased (i.e., increasing order of approximation to English).

Let us decide that for a reasonably large corpus, if the frequency of occurrence of a letter in a context of k letters is above a certain threshold, the string of these $k + 1$ letters has the structure of English, while if it is below the threshold this string may not appear in English. We can now replace the stochastic description with a finite automaton. In the state graph of this automaton all authorized sequences of k letters correspond to a state. With the string $a_{i_1} a_{i_2} \cdots a_{i_k}$ we associate the state $S(a_{i_1}, a_{i_2}, \ldots, a_{i_k})$. If this string authorizes the letter $a_{i_{k+1}}$ to occur on its right, we will consider the state $S(a_{i_2} a_{i_3} \cdots a_{i_{k+1}})$, and draw an edge, labeled $a_{1_{k+1}}$, from $S(a_{i_1} a_{i_2} \cdots a_{i_k})$ to $S(a_{i_2} a_{i_3} \cdots a_{i_{k+1}})$. This procedure provides the complete state graph. We choose the states corresponding to strings starting with blanks [i.e., all $S(\# a_{j_1} \cdots a_{j_{k-1}})$] as initial states and the states ending with blanks [i.e., all $S(a_{p_1} \cdots a_{p_{k-1}} \#)$] as final states.

This device generates not only words of English, but also English-like sequences, including strings such as *termission*, *ponsider*, and so on, which look like English words and can be pronounced consistently and without hesitation by English speakers. The device should not generate a string such as *tmisresnoi* (made of the same letters as *termission*), since, as English speakers agree, it is not English-like. The graph is thus not only a model of the performance of an English speaker, but also a model of his competence. The described structure is not restricted to words in the lexicon of English, since it corresponds to all sequences that might be English, were there no accidental restrictions on the size and use of the lexicon.

[5] A. A. Markov, "Essai d'une recherche statistique sur le texte du roman *Eugène Onéguine*," *Bull. Acad. Impériale des Sciences de Saint-Pétersbourg*, 1913–1917.

[6] C. Shannon, "Prediction and Entropy in Printed English," *Bell. System Tech. J.*, vol. 30 (1951), 50–64.

VII

Context-Free Languages

In earlier chapters we have recognized a number of
regularities occurring in strings of natural languages
(for example, distribution of noun phrases, (§5.3.1).
Now we shall examine a class of devices that formally
represents these regularities.

7.1

Constituent Analysis
of Natural Languages

Sentences are factorized into words or phrases, such phrases being refactorized
into other phrases and/or words. Words are decomposed into morphemes
and/or phonemes, morphemes into phonemes. The main practical device
used both to recognize the elementary units and to determine their arrangement is a "commutation" or "substitution" test.

Assume that a sentence S_1 has the form $t\,a\,g$, that there are linguistic
reasons for dividing it into these three segments, and that another sentence,
S_2 has the shape $h\,b\,k$. We then commute a and b. If the resulting $t\,b\,g$ and
$h\,a\,k$ are sentences, we say that a and b belong to the same grammatical
category.

For example, suppose we have

$S_1 = $ *John saw the girl*
$S_2 = $ *This mother was proud of him*

with $t = $ *John*; $a = $ *saw*; $g = $ *the girl*; $h = $ *this mother*; $b = $ *was proud of*; $k = $ *him*. The results $t\ b\ g$ and $h\ a\ k$ are

John was proud of the girl,
This mother saw him.

Both are correct sentences. But if we analyze S_1 as above, and S_2 as follows:

$h = $ *This mother;* $b = $ *was proud;* $k = $ *of him*

the result of the commutation test is

John was proud the girl,
This mother saw of him.

Neither is a correct sentence. We conclude from these tests that *saw* and *was proud of* belong to a common category, which we will call verb (V).

If we now analyze S_1 as ag ($a = $ *John*), or ta ($a = $ *the girl*), and S_2 as bk ($b = $ *this mother*), or hb ($b = $ *him*), and if we perform the commutation test on any two of these analyses, we conclude that the four elements *John, the girl, this mother, him* belong to a common category, which we will call noun phrase (NP). We can continue to examine such categories with the same test. In NP positions, we observe strings of the type

Npr   (proper name)
Det N   (determiner, noun)
Det Adj N   (determiner, adjective, noun)
Det (Adj) (Adj)* and Adj N.

These last three can be adjoined strings of the types

(whom + which + that) NP V
(whom + which + that) V (e + NP)
prep (whom + which) NP V, . . .

—that is, strings of the category relative clause (*RelCl*). We can thus write such statements as:

NP   can be   *Npr*
NP   can be   *Det N*
. . . .
NP   can be   *Det Adj N RelCl*
NP   can be   *Det (Adj) (Adj)* and Adj N RelCl,*

Though the procedure just stated must be modified in certain cases,[1] as a first approximation to the description of sequences, we can see that it leads to statements of the form

$$A \quad \text{can be} \quad \psi$$

where A is a grammatical category, and ψ a sequence of such categories and/or of words such as the conjunction *and*. In such statements, if we replace the term "can be" by the arrow $\rightarrow$, with the meaning defined for it in Chapter II, we have a set of rewriting rules. We choose S (for "sentence," the aim of syntactic description) as the axiom. We have an auxiliary (i.e., nonterminal) vocabulary V_A containing category names (S, V, *Npr*, *NP*, and so on), and a terminal vocabulary V_T containing the set of words and morphemes of the language[2] described.

Rules of the type

$$A \rightarrow \varphi, \qquad A \in V_A, \qquad \varphi \in (V_A \cup V_T)^*,$$

are called context-free rules or Chomsky rules (C-rules), after the linguist who recognized their importance for linguistic theory. Grammars with rules of this type will be called C-grammars, and the corresponding languages, C-languages.

7.2

Examples of C-grammars

EXAMPLE I

The definitions we gave of K-rule, and of K-grammar, fulfill the conditions that define C-rules and C-grammars. K-languages are thus C-languages.

EXAMPLE II

$$V_A = \{S\}, \qquad V_T = \{a, b\}$$

$$(G_1) \quad \begin{vmatrix} S \rightarrow aSb \\ S \rightarrow ab. \end{vmatrix}$$

---

[1] We will mention later some of the problems raised by an analysis in contiguous segments as performed here—particularly the notion of discontinuous constituent (Chapter VIII).

[2] Such substitution procedures are also used to determine the set of morphemes of the language and the set of its phonemes.

The language $L(G_1)$ is the set $\{a^n b^n : n > 0\}$. In the preceding chapter we showed that this language is not a K-language. The class of K-languages, therefore, is properly included in the class of C-languages.

EXAMPLE III _____

$$(G_2) \quad \begin{array}{|l} S \to aSb \\ S \to aS \\ S \to bT \\ T \to bT \\ T \to e. \end{array}$$

The grammar (G_2) generates a K-language $\{a^p b^q : p \geqslant 0, q > 0\}$, although it contains a proper C-rule (i.e., $S \to aSb$). The rules are such that the C-rule, in conjunction with the other rules of the grammar, generates twice a subset of the language $L(G_2)$. In fact, the last four rules alone are sufficient to generate $L(G_2)$. In a way, then, the C-rule is superfluous, which explains why $L(G_2)$ is a K-language. In general, detecting superfluous rules is extremely difficult.

EXAMPLE IV _____

$$V_A = \{S, T\}, \qquad V_T = \{a, c\},$$

$$(G_3) \quad \begin{array}{|l} S \to TT \\ T \to aTa \\ T \to c. \end{array}$$

We derive a string

$$S \to TT \to aTaT \to acaT \to acaaTa$$
$$\to acaaaTaa \to acaaacaa.$$

The language generated by (G_3) is

$$L(G_3) = \{a^p ca^{p+q} ca^q : p, q \geqslant 0\}.$$

7.3

_____

Derivations and Trees

The single auxiliary symbol in the left member of a C-rule allows a particular representation of its functioning. For each rule $A \to BC \cdots KL$, $A \in V_A$; $B, C, \ldots K, L \in V_A \cup V_T$, we can draw a treelike graph, the root of which is labeled A. Edges connect A to each of the left-to-right ordered nodes:

B, C, . . . , K, L (Figure 7.1). Each of the symbols *B, C, . . . , K, L* used on the left side of a C-rule also has a corresponding tree branching from it (Figure 7.2).

Trees are associated with derivations. A derivation represents all substitutions performed by the rules in generating a string. For most if not

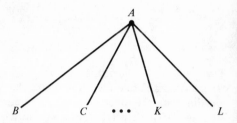

FIGURE 7.1

all linguistic purposes, derivations indicate details of the building process irrelevant to the structure of the string. The problem is that a single string may be produced by many different derivations, indicative of a single substitution pattern and thus represented by a single tree.

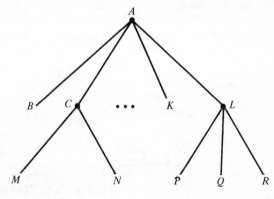

FIGURE 7.2

Nonterminal nodes *B, M, N, . . . , K, P, Q, R* may branch again. When all nonbranching nodes are terminal, the resulting derived word is obtained by reading the terminal nodes from left to right.

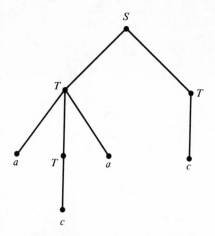

FIGURE 7.3

For example, the following derivations of the grammar (G_3) above correspond to a single string and a single tree (Figure 7.3).

$$S \to TT \to aTaT \to acaT \to acac,$$

$$S \to TT \to Tc \to aTac \to acac,$$

$$S \to TT \to aTaT \to aTac \to acac.$$

At each step we can replace any of the auxiliary symbols by applying the corresponding rule. This allows different derivations with the same final result. Thus, trees can be considered as representing equivalence classes of derivations.

7.4

Ambiguity

In some cases the alternative derivations of a given string can be associated with different trees. We say that such strings are ambiguous with respect to the grammar that generates them.

EXAMPLE I _____

Using the grammar (G_2) above, we can derive the string *aabb* as follows:

$$S \to aSb \to aaSb \to aabTb \to aabb,$$
$$S \to aS \to aaS \to aabT \to aabbT \to aabb.$$

Two different trees are associated with these derivations (Figure 7.4).

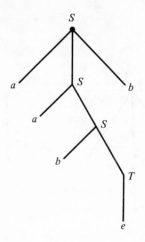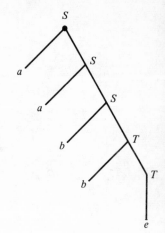

FIGURE 7.4

EXAMPLE II _____

$$V_A = \{S, T\}, \qquad V_T = \{a, b\}$$

(G_a)
$$\begin{aligned}
S &\to TT \\
T &\to aTa \\
T &\to bTb \\
T &\to e, \qquad L(G_a) = \{x\tilde{x}y\tilde{y}: x, y \in V_T^*\}^3.
\end{aligned}$$

We can derive the string *aaaaaa* (a^6) by two different paths:

$$S \to TT \to aTaT \to aaT \to aaaTa \to aaaaTaa \to a^6,$$
$$S \to TT \to TaTa \to Taa \to aTaaa \to aaTaaaa \to a^6,$$

with which we associate the different trees in Figure 7.5.

Ambiguity originates in many ways. It may arise from superfluous rules, as in Example I. If we suppress the first rule of (G_2), the generated language $L(G_2)$ remains unchanged, but the string a^2b^2 is no longer ambiguous. It now has only the right tree of Figure 7.5. No other string of $L(G_2)$ is ambiguous. Thus, there are languages that are ambiguous with respect to a given C-grammar but not with respect to some other C-grammar.

Example II is different. It can be shown that the language $L(G_a)$ will be ambiguous regardless of the C-grammar used to generate it. In such circumstances the language is said to be inherently ambiguous.

---

[3] We recall that if x is string, $\tilde{x}$ is its mirror image. The letters of $\tilde{x}$ read from left to right are the letters of x read from right to left.

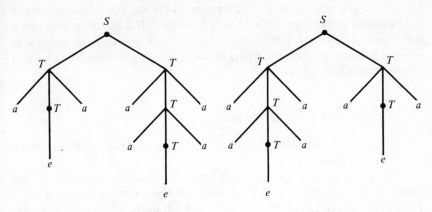

FIGURE 7.5

7.5

Description of C-grammars

7.5.1
SELF-EMBEDDING GRAMMARS

The difference in descriptive power of C-rules and K-rules is a result of the less restricted shape of C-rules. In C-derivations an auxiliary symbol may occur with nonnull strings on each side; this is not the case for K-derivations (§ 6.2.3). In this light we can observe various patterns relevant to the description of natural languages.

When we have a rule such as

$$A \to uBv; \quad A, B \in V_A; \quad u, v \in (V_T \cup V_A)^* \setminus e,$$

the auxiliary symbol B can be the starting point of a derivation. The symbol B then heads a certain construction, and we say that the construction B is nested, or embedded, into the construction A. If, moreover, we have a rule $B \to xCy$ with x and y again nonnull, C is nested or embedded into B, and into A. This process may continue. If there exists a symbol A such that we have

$$A \to u_1 A_1 v_1 \to \cdots \to u_k A v_k,$$

$u_k \neq e, v_k \neq e$, and A recurs after a certain number of steps, we say that A is a self-embedding symbol. Corresponding grammars are called self-embedding grammars.

If a C-grammar generates a language that is not a K-language, then it must contain at least one self-embedding symbol. If a grammar contains a self-embedding symbol, it does not obligatorily generate a C-language that is not a K-language: grammar (G_2) above, with the self-embedding symbol S, generates a K-language.

7.5.2
CLASSES OF C-GRAMMARS

It is possible to define various classes of C-grammars, according to the shapes ψ of C-rules $A \rightarrow \psi$.

We have already used rules in which $\psi = e$, thus allowing the null string e to be a member of a C-language. We can also have $\psi = B \in V_A$. These two types of rules, $A \rightarrow e$ and $A \rightarrow B$, up to the string e, do not contribute directly to the formation of the strings of C-languages. In fact, given a grammar (G) with rules that generate $L(G)$, it is always possible to associate with (G) a grammar (G'), without any rule of the types $A \rightarrow e$ and $A \rightarrow B$, and such that $L(G') = L(G)$ (up to the string e).

C-rules of the form $\psi = \alpha B\beta$, α, $\beta \in V_T^*$ (i.e., with a right member containing only one auxiliary symbol) are called linear rules. Grammars made of such rules (and of terminal rules) are called *linear grammars*.

Consider the following examples:

$$(G_p) \quad \begin{vmatrix} S \rightarrow aSS \\ S \rightarrow b \end{vmatrix} \quad \text{and} \quad (G_m) \quad \begin{vmatrix} S \rightarrow AAA \\ A \rightarrow aAb \\ A \rightarrow ab. \end{vmatrix}$$

The steps in derivations of (G_p) may contain arbitrarily many occurrences of auxiliary symbols (here, occurrences of S). For (G_m) this number is at most 3.

Finite products of linear languages are called metalinear languages. Their grammars, obtained as in § 7.7.1.1, are called *metalinear grammars*. A whole range of special grammars have been defined for linguistic and computational purposes.

In linguistics, grammars limited to rules of the two forms $A \rightarrow BC$ and $A \rightarrow a$ have been used for binary constituent analysis. These grammars are called *normal grammars*.

Programming languages are often partially described with C-grammars. A program—a string of a programming language—is analyzed by the computer in terms of the rules of a C-grammar. Performing efficient computations requires special forms of rules. Syntactic analysis can be simplified with *sequential grammars*, for example. These grammars have rules that can be applied only in a certain order in a derivation. A given rule may be applied several times, but once it has been used, it cannot be used any longer.

Another device may consist of marking the rules, requiring that each contains, for example, a terminal symbol not appearing in any other rule. In this way, given a string of the corresponding language, it is easy to enumerate directly the rules used in its derivation.

7.5.3
REPRESENTATIONS OF STRUCTURES

Interpreting C-rules in terms of trees provides us with a way of representing the structure of the generated strings. The most common interpretation is that A, in a rule $A \rightarrow \psi$, indicates a category, and that ψ indicates a way of building elements of this category. ψ is a sequence of elements that constitute a member of the category when concatenated. There are other formal ways of representing this string structure.

7.5.3.1
LABELED BRACKETING

If the sequence ψ is a string belonging to the category A, we can write $[_A\psi_A]$ instead. The matching square brackets are indexed by the name of the category. In a C-grammar, since auxiliary symbols all correspond to categories, we can modify the form of the rules, writing for each of them $A \rightarrow [_A\psi_A]$ instead of $A \rightarrow \psi$. We consider the labeled brackets as additional terminal symbols, and we use the new grammar to derive strings in which the constituent structure is directly marked. Because there is a one-to-one correspondence between opening ([) and closing (]) brackets, we can dispense with one of the two labels.

EXAMPLE _____

Consider grammar (G_3):

$$S \rightarrow TT, \quad T \rightarrow aTa, \quad T \rightarrow c \, .$$

We modify it so that

$$S \rightarrow [_STT], \quad T \rightarrow [_TaTa], \quad T \rightarrow [_Tc].$$

The result of the derivation

$$S \rightarrow [_STT] \rightarrow [_S[_TaTa]T] \rightarrow [_S[_Ta[_Tc]a]T] \rightarrow [_S[_Ta[_Tc]a][_Tc]]$$

corresponds to the tree of Figure 7.3 above.

7.5.3.2
POLISH NOTATION

Certain types of C-rules allow representation of structures under a different interpretation of the rules.

We suppose that we are dealing again with constituents. Constituents are either basic (i.e., terminal) and named $a_1, a_2, \ldots, a_m$, or compound and named $f_1, f_2, \ldots, f_n$. We can suppose that the compound constituents we are dealing with are all k-ary (i.e., composed of k simpler constituents). If the string $f_i a_{j_1} a_{j_2} \cdots a_{j_k}$ is such a constituent, it is called f_i. It can again be combined with $k - 1$ basic or compound constituents to constitute a new compound constituent f_l. This process can be iterated at will. The set of strings that corresponds to these expressions can be described with a C-grammar.

Let S be any such constituent.

1. If S is basic, we write

$$S \rightarrow a_j: \qquad 1 \leqslant j \leqslant m.$$

2. If S is compound, we write

$$S \rightarrow f_i S^k \quad : \quad 1 \leqslant i \leqslant m,$$

with $V_A = \{S\}$ and $V_T = \{f_i, a_j : 1 \leqslant i \leqslant m, 1 \leqslant j \leqslant n\}$.

The preceding rules constitute a C-grammar that generates our set of expressions.

The grammar

$$S \rightarrow bSS, \qquad S \rightarrow a$$

generates binary constituents ($k = 2$), all of type b.

*7.5.4
ALGEBRAIC EQUATIONS

Let us change the notation for C-grammars. Whenever the auxiliary symbol A is the left member of the rules

$$A \rightarrow f_1, \quad A \rightarrow f_2, \quad \ldots, \quad A \rightarrow f_k,$$

we replace this list of rules by the equation

$$A = f_1 + f_2 + \cdots + f_k,$$

where arrows are replaced with an "equal" sign, and the "plus" sign is approximately equivalent to "or." We now have more than a simple change of notations. If a C-grammar uses n auxiliary symbols, it can in fact be considered as a system of n equations in n variables (the elements of V_A).

Many computations classical for ordinary equations can be performed, the only difference being that the products of elements (of V_A and V_T) are not commutative as in classical algebra.

For example, we can solve equations by successive approximations. We associate the equation

(E) $\quad S = aSa + c \quad$ with the C-grammar $\quad S \to aSa; \quad S \to c.$

We replace, in the right member of (E), the variable S with a zero, which yields $S^{(0)}$, the zero-order approximation:

$S^{(0)} = c.$

We now replace S with $S^{(0)}$ in the right member of (E), obtaining the first-order approximation:

$S^{(1)} = aca + c.$

In the same way, we have

$$S^{(2)} = a(aca + c)a + c = a^2ca^2 + aca + a$$

.

.

.

$$S^{(n)} = a^nca^n + \cdots + aca + c = \sum_{i=0}^{i=n} a^ica^i.$$

The solution is $S^{(\infty)}$, given by the formal power series in noncommutative variables:

$$S^{(\infty)} = \sum_{i=0}^{i=\infty} a^ica^i.$$

The union of the terms (i.e., the support) of $S^{(\infty)}$ constitutes the language generated by the grammar. In the general case of a system of n equations, the solution is a set of n formal power series, each associated to an auxiliary symbol. The language of the corresponding grammar is still the support of $S^{(\infty)}$, S being the axiom.

When, in the successive approximation process, several identical words occur in a sum, they add together. Then a numerical coefficient that counts the occurrences of a word is attached to it, directly providing the degree of ambiguity of the word with respect to the grammar.

We have, for example,

$$S = aaSaa + aSa + c$$

$$S^{(0)} = c$$

$$S^{(1)} = a^2ca^2 + aca + c$$

$$S^{(2)} = a^2(a^2ca^2 + aca + c)a^2 + a(a^2ca^2 + aca + c)a + c$$

$$= a^4ca^4 + 2a^3ca^3 + 2a^2ca^2 + aca + c.$$

It is easy to verify that the words a^3ca^3 and a^2ca^2 are ambiguous with respect to the corresponding grammar.

Not only do equations constitute a compact and natural way of displaying C-grammars, but, as M. P. Schützenberger has shown, they also have deep mathematical properties that link the framework of noncommutative power series to the classical algebraic functions.

7.6

A Language That Is Not a C-language

It can be shown, as we did for K-languages (§ 6.2.4), that the language $L = \{a^n b^n c^n : n > 0\}$ is not a C-language. One can prove that any C-grammar that can generate L produces preterminal lines of derivation of the form $a^k b^l G c^m$, where G is an auxiliary symbol that heads self-embedding derivations:

$$G \to \cdots \to b^r G c^s \to \cdots \to b^{ir} G c^{is} \to \cdots$$

and terminating ones:

$$G \to b^p c^q.$$

Thus, from the preterminal string $a^k b^l G c^m$, whenever it is possible to derive $a^k b^k c^k \in L$, it is possible to derive at the same time an infinite number of terminal strings not in L.

7.7

Formal Properties

7.7.1
CLOSURE PROPERTIES

The family of C-languages is closed under union, product, and star. It is not closed under intersection (nor under complementation, by De-Morgan's law). We will prove these statements.

7.7.1.1
UNION AND PRODUCT OF TWO C-LANGUAGES

We consider two C-grammars (G_1) and (G_2), defined on two disjoint[4] auxiliary vocabularies, with axioms S_1 and S_2, respectively. We choose a new axiom S not in either of the two auxiliary vocabularies, and we build new grammars composed of (G_1) and (G_2) (i.e., union of vocabularies, union of the sets of rules).

If we now add the rules

$$S \to S_1, \qquad S \to S_2$$

to the union of rules, we obtain a grammar that generates the union $L(G_1) \cup L(G_2)$, and this new grammar is a C-grammar.

If, instead of the previous two rules, we add the rule

$$S \to S_1 S_2$$

to the union of the rules of (G_1) and (G_2), we obtain a C-grammar that generates the product $L(G_1)L(G_2)$.

7.7.1.2
STAR LANGUAGE AND MIRROR LANGUAGE OF A C-LANGUAGE

Let (G) be a C-grammar with axiom S. We choose a new auxiliary symbol T as the axiom of the grammar made of the rules of (G), to which we add the two rules

$$T \to TS, \qquad T \to e.$$

---

[4] This is not a restriction; if in all rules of a C-grammar we replace the name of a symbol A of V_A by another name B not already in V_A, the language and the shape of the trees generated by the C-grammar are not changed.

This new grammar is a C-grammar that generates the union of the languages $\{e\}, L(G), (L(G))^2, \ldots, (L(G))^n, \ldots$, namely the star language of $L(G)$.

Given a C-grammar (G) and its language $L(G)$, we can consider its mirror image $\widetilde{L(G)}$. This language can be obtained by transforming (G) into $(\widetilde{G})$. The grammar $(\widetilde{G})$ has for rules $\{A \rightarrow \tilde{\psi}\}$, where $\{A \rightarrow \psi\}$ are the rules of (G).

7.7.2
INTERSECTION

We show here that the intersection of two C-languages is generally not a C-language, giving an example where this situation arises.

Consider the C-languages

$$L_1 = \{a^m b^m a^p : m, p \geqslant 0\},$$

$$L_2 = \{a^q b^n a^n : q, n \geqslant 0\}.$$

Their grammars are, respectively,

$$(G_1) \quad \begin{vmatrix} S_1 \rightarrow T_1 U_1 \\ T_1 \rightarrow a T_1 b \\ T_1 \rightarrow e \\ U_1 \rightarrow U_1 a \\ U_1 \rightarrow e \end{vmatrix} \qquad (G_2) \quad \begin{vmatrix} S_2 \rightarrow T_2 U_2 \\ T_2 \rightarrow a T_2 \\ T_2 \rightarrow e \\ U_2 \rightarrow b U_2 a \\ U_2 \rightarrow e. \end{vmatrix}$$

The intersection of their languages is

$$L_1 \cap L_2 = \{a^n b^n a^n : n \geqslant 0\}.$$

As indicated above ($\S 7.6$), this language is not a C-language.

Related to this is a theorem.

Theorem

The intersection of a C-language with a K-language is a C-language.

7.8

Push-down Storage Automata

Just as Turing machines correspond to rewriting systems, and finite automata to K-grammars, so can we associate a family of abstract machines, called push-down storage automata, to the class of C-grammars.

7.8.1
DEFINITIONS

A push-down storage automaton (p.d.s. automaton) has both an input tape and an output tape (Figure 7.6). It can read only the input. The output component includes a reading-writing head, capable also of erasing symbols in such a way that all and only blanks appear on one given side of the head, and an output or memory tape that can move in both directions.

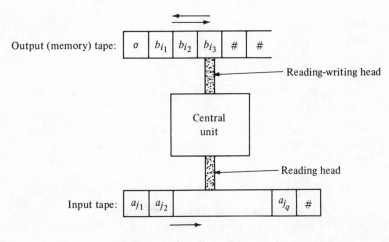

FIGURE 7.6

Input strings are defined on $A = \{a_i : 1 \leqslant i \leqslant m\}$, and input tapes read in the finite-automaton mode.

Only half the output tape is used. It starts with a special symbol σ, and it provisionally stores strings on $B = \{b_j : 1 \leqslant j \leqslant n\}$. These output strings occupy the space between σ, the end of the tape, and the output head, to the right of which an indefinite supply of tape is available. As the memory tape is moved to the right, erasure takes place.

The central unit has a finite set of states $\sum = \{S_k : 0 \leqslant k \leqslant p\}$ with a subset of final states $\Sigma_f \subset \Sigma$ distinguished as usual.

Instructions are of the type

$$(a_i, S_j, b_k) \rightarrow (S_l, 0).$$

A situation consists in a state S_j and the two symbols a_i, b_k under the heads. In initial and final situations, the special symbol σ occurs under the output head. An instruction changes the state from S_j to S_l, and moves the input tape one square left. The output O is either $b_m \in B$ printed on the memory tape, in which case the tape is moved one square left, or the erasure symbol R, in which case the tape is moved one square right, the blank symbol $\#$ replacing b_k on the tape. When we allow the symbol e in the position(s) a_i and/or b_k, no move of the corresponding tape(s) takes place.

Computations start in an initial state S_0 on the leftmost symbol of the input tape. The output head is on σ, and the rest of the output tape is blank. An input string is accepted when the computation ends in a state of Σ_f, with the input entirely read and the memory tape blank (i.e., the head on σ). The set of the accepted strings is the language accepted by the automaton.

EXAMPLE

$$A = \{a, b\}, \quad B = \{c\}, \quad \Sigma = \{S_0, S_1\}, \quad \Sigma_f = \{S_1\}.$$

The instructions are

$$(a, S_0, \sigma) \rightarrow (S_1, c)$$
$$(a, S_1, c) \rightarrow (S_1, c)$$
$$(b, S_1, c) \rightarrow (S_1, R).$$

The language accepted by the automaton is $L = \{a^n b^n : n > 0\}$, a C-language (Figure 7.7).

As usual with automata, the definitions can be extended.

1. P.d.s. automata can be deterministic or not.
2. For the output O we can allow a string $x \in B^*$, instead of only single elements of B. Then, the tape will move $d^0(x)$ squares to the left.
3. Instructions can be interpreted differently. Instead of "recognizing" strings, the automaton could "produce" strings. The computations would start as before, but with a blank input tape, and the situations (a_i, S_j, b_k) would read: In state S_j, reading b_k, the automaton prints a_i on the input tape. The rest of the instruction is interpreted as before (such an example is given in § 7.8.2 below).

These various modifications can also be combined.

7.8.2
EQUIVALENCE WITH C-GRAMMARS

Though rigorous proofs of the equivalence between C-grammars and p.d.s. automata can be given,[5] we will only indicate how a nondeterministic

---

[5] N. Chomsky, "Formal Properties of Grammars," in D. Luce, R. R. Bush, and E. Galenter, eds., *Handbook of Mathematical Psychology*, vol. II (New York: John Wiley & Sons, Inc., 1963) chap. 12; G. H. Matthews, "Discontinuity and Asymmetry in Phrase Structure Grammars," *Information and Control*, vol. VI (1963), pp. 137–146; M. P. Schützenberger, "On Context-Free Languages and Push-Down Automata," *Information and Control*, vol. VI (1963), 246–264.

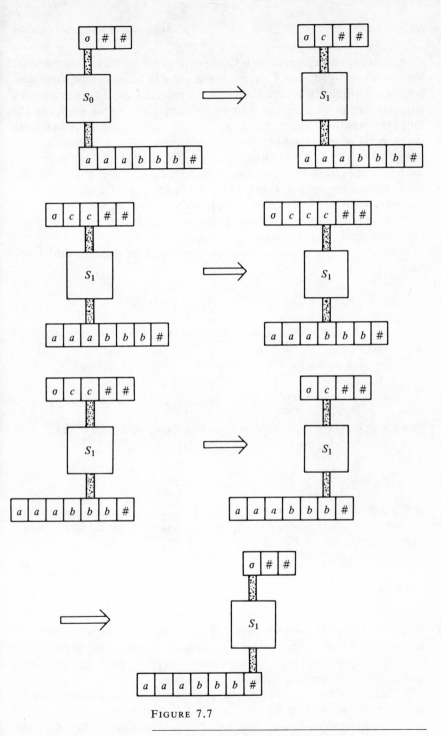

FIGURE 7.7

The automaton accepts the string a^3b^3.

p.d.s. automaton can generate a C-language given by its C-grammar. We have mentioned that for a C-grammar the order in which the auxiliary symbols are rewritten in a derivation has no influence on the corresponding terminal string. We can, for example, systematically derive strings in the following way. By always rewriting the rightmost auxiliary symbol, until the terminal string is reached, all strings of the derivation have the form Yx, $Y \in (V_A \cup V_T)^*$, $x \in V_T^*$. Given a string Yx, the part x undergoes no further modification during subsequent derivation, while Y will become terminal from the right. It is easy to build a producing p.d.s. automaton that performs this type of derivation. The strings are placed on the memory tape. When a terminal part appears (next to the head), it is transferred to the input tape (and erased from the memory tape).

With each rule $A \rightarrow \psi$ of the given C-grammar we associate the instruction

$$(e, S_w, A) \rightarrow (S_w, \psi)$$

which has no effect on the input tape. In state S_w the automaton writes on the memory tape.

For each element $a_i \in V_T$ we have the transfer instruction

$$(a_i, S_w, a_i) \rightarrow (S_w, R)$$

that places a_i on the input tape and erases it from the memory tape.

Computations start with the instruction

$$(\#, S_0, \sigma) \rightarrow (S_w, S)$$

that places the axiom S of the grammar on the memory tape and switches the automaton from initial state S_0 to S_w. Computations end in a situation $(a\#_i, S_w, \sigma)$.

7.8.3
REMARKS

The term "push-down" refers to the special form of memory. It is essentially a stack whose bottom is σ. New elements can be introduced only on the "top," and erasures take place only at the "top." If an erasure has to take place in the "middle" of the memory, everything between the symbols to be erased and the head must also be erased.

In finite automata, "finite" refers to the size of the memory, which is strictly finite, since there are a finite number of states that can be used to recall information about input strings. In this sense, push-down automata are not finite, since the memory used in computations consists both of a memory string and a state (or finite pattern of states). Since memory strings are potentially unbounded, p.d.s. automata are infinite automata. Notice that if we put an a priori limit on the length of the memory tape available, without modifying the functioning mode, the device is equivalent to a finite automaton whose states correspond to the pairs *memory string, state,* now finite in number. This observation is related to self-embedding, the property that distinguishes C-languages from K-languages.

We can describe self-embedding in terms of "constraints." Given a word

$$f = a_{i_1} a_{i_2} \cdots a_{i_{p-1}} a_{i_p}$$

the constraints between the elements a_i's can be finite or infinite (§ 5.3.1). Finite constraints can be described by finite automata. There are many types of infinite constraints.

Suppose we are dealing with a language that has some infinite constraints between a_{i_1} and a_{i_p}, and between a_{i_2} and $a_{i_{p-1}}$ (Figure 7.8). The

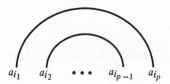

FIGURE 7.8

string $a_{i_2} \cdots a_{i_{p-1}}$ is embedded into the string f. Between a_{i_2} and $a_{i_{p-1}}$ we could have other constraints nested one into the other. If the language is such that only a fixed number of constraints can be nested in this way, the constraints can be described by finite automata. If, instead, we can have an unbounded number of constraints nested one within the other, as occurs with self-embedded languages, then we must use a p.d.s. automaton for their description. The automaton will be used approximately as follows.

When it computes the structure of Figure 7.9, the automaton reads the input string $a_{i_1} \cdots a_{i_{2q}}$, simultaneously storing the symbols $a_{i_1} a_{i_2} \cdots a_{i_{q-1}}$ on the memory tape in this order. When it reads a_q, the symbol $a_{i_{q-1}}$ is under the output head, allowing it to check the corresponding constraint; $a_{i_{q-1}}$ is then erased. The automaton now reads $a_{i_{q-1}}$ on the output tape and $a_{i_{q+1}}$ on the input tape. Since these symbols are also constrained, $a_{i_{q-2}}$ is erased and the input tape moved to the left. From then on the automaton can check pairs of constrained symbols, until it checks the pair $a_{i_{2q}}, a_{i_1}$. At this point

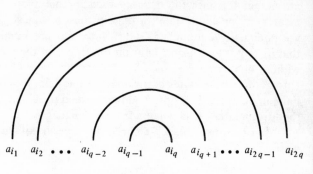

FIGURE 7.9

the memory tape is empty, and the input string has been read completely. That the string $a_{i_1} a_{i_2} \cdots a_{i_{q-1}}$ can be of unbounded length requires a potentially infinite memory. In § 7.9.2 we will see that though the patterns of constraints in C-languages seem more general, they are essentially compounded patterns of the type in Figure 7.9.

*7.9

_____

Algebraic Characterization

Just as certain algebraic systems are associated with rewriting systems and K-languages, M. P. Schützenberger has also described C-languages in terms of algebraic operations on sets.

7.9.1
DYCK LANGUAGES

We will first consider a family of remarkable sets. Let

$$A = \{x_i, x_{-i} : 1 \leqslant i \leqslant n\}$$

be an alphabet of $2n$ letters paired by indices of opposite signs. We consider the set A^* and define a transformation on its words. If $f \in A^*$ is of one of the forms $\alpha x_i x_{-i} \beta$, $\alpha x_{-i} x_i \beta$, we will say that f reduces to $\alpha\beta$, canceling two consecutive letters with identical index and opposite signs. We apply to f the rewriting rules

$$x_i x_{-i} \rightarrow e, \qquad x_{-i} x_i \rightarrow e \qquad \text{for all } i.$$

We reapply the operation to the result of a reduction such as $\alpha\beta$ until the resulting string cannot be further reduced.

EXAMPLE

The word $x_1 y_{-1} y_1 x_{-1} x_2$ reduces to $x_1 x_{-1} x_2$, then to x_2.

The word $x_1 x_{-1} x_1 x_{-1}$ reduces variously by canceling the rightmost part $x_1 x_{-1}$, the leftmost part $x_1 x_{-1}$, or the central part $x_{-1} x_1$. In any case, the result is

$$x_{-1} x_1$$

which, in turn, reduces to e.

It can be shown that the order in which pairs of letters are reduced inside a word does not affect the final result of reduction.

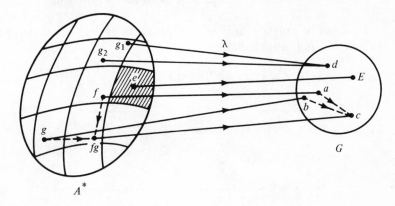

FIGURE 7.10

λ is the morphism between A^* and the free group G. The classes of A^* are shown; in one of them we have $\lambda(g_1) = \lambda(g_2) = d$. Dotted arrows indicate product is within sets—for example,

$$\lambda(fg) = \lambda(f)\lambda(g) = (ab) = c$$

The reduction rules thus define over A^* a set of equivalence classes. The reduction operation is a morphism that maps A^* onto the set of equivalence classes. This set is a group G, called the "free group" on the generators $\{x_i : 1 \leqslant i \leqslant n\}$. We thus have the picture given in Figure 7.10. The null word e of A^* has E for image in G. $\lambda(e) = E$ is the unit element of G. The set $\lambda^{-1}(E)$, the class of words of A^* that reduce to e, is called a Dyck language, denoted by D^*. (D^* corresponds to the crosshatched class in Figure 7.10.) This language is the basis of the algebraic definition of C-languages.

7.9.2
ALGEBRAIC DEFINITION

A C-language will be defined by:

1. A Dyck language D^* on an alphabet A, as above.
2. A set of restrictions on certain words of D^*:
    (a) restrictions on initial letters, retaining the words of D^* that start only with certain letters, and indicating a set $I \subset A$ of authorized initial letters; and
    (b) interdiction of certain transitions between letters, given by a set $J \subset A^2$. We retain the words of D^* that are not of the form $\alpha x_i x_j \beta$, $x_i x_j \in J$.
3. A coding of the letters of A in terms of words on the alphabet V_T of the C-language—that is, a morphism μ of A^* into V_T^*.

It can be proven that if L is a C-language on V_T, it is always possible to find D^*, I, J, μ such that

$$L = \mu(D^* \cap IA^* \cap A^* \setminus A^*JA^*)$$

EXAMPLE _____

Let $L = \{a^{2p}ca^p : p \geqslant 0\}$. We choose

$$A = \{x_1, x_{-1}, x_2, x_{-2}\}$$
$$I = \{x_1\}$$
$$J = \{x_1 x_{-1}, x_1 x_{-2}, x_{-1} x_1, x_{-1} x_2, x_{-1} x_{-2}, x_2 x_1, x_2 x_2, x_{-2} x_1, x_{-2} x_2, x_{-2} x_{-2}\}.$$

$$\mu : \quad \begin{vmatrix} x_1 \to aa \\ x_{-1} \to a \\ x_2 \to c \\ x_{-2} \to e. \end{vmatrix}$$

7.9.3
EQUIVALENCE BETWEEN C-GRAMMARS
AND ALGEBRAIC SYSTEMS

We will not give a formal proof of equivalence but will make more apparent the relations between the two devices. If we consider C-grammars whose rules have one of the forms

$$A \to aBC \cdots Kb = a\alpha b$$

$$A \to ab$$

$$A, B, C, \ldots, K \in V_A; \quad \alpha \in V_A^*; \quad a, b \in V_T$$

we can interpret each of these rules as representing a constraint that links *a* and *b*. In fact the trees associated with these types of rules include edges between *a* and *b* that can be looked upon as an arch linking both letters (Figure 7.11). The symbols *B, C, . . . , K* in turn bring similar arches. Thus, a word generated by such C-rules will have a structure indicated by arches. Returning now to the words of *D**, if we link with arches the letters that together cancel, we obtain exactly the same patterns of arches. The structures

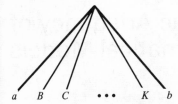 

FIGURE 7.11

of the words of *D** and the words of the special C-grammars we considered are identical. The restrictions that we defined on *D** are also found in the grammars.

1. The axiom *S* is a left member of certain rules $S \to aB \cdots b$; the *a*'s that occur in these rules will begin all the words of the C-language, and correspond to the set *I*.

2. In a rule $A \to a\alpha b$, the sequence of auxiliary symbols α is generally restricted (i.e., not all combinations may appear). The environment of *B* and *C* ($\alpha = BC \cdots K$), which are themselves left members of rules such as $B \to aDb$, $C \to cd$, imposes conditions on the sequence of terminals. In this example the transition *bc* is allowed but others are not. The set *J* corresponds to this situation.

3. In the C-grammars we are comparing with algebraic systems, we distinguished letters (*a, b,* and so on) rather than strings, we could generalize the rules to allow strings (*f, g,* and so on) in their positions. This yields the morphism (here, $a \to f$, $b \to g$, and so on).

The proof of the equivalence consists in building special types of C-grammars that resemble the one mentioned. The construction starts from any C-grammar, and it does not change the generated language.

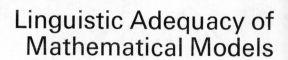

Linguistic Adequacy of
Mathematical Models

The form of a model depends on the nature of the
data it will account for. In this chapter we will
examine how the mathematical models we have
described handle linguistic facts under various
hypotheses about the general shape of the data.

8.1

Natural Languages
Characterized as Sets of Strings

We could consider that the object of a linguistic description is to sort out
the grammatical strings from the ungrammatical strings. Such a grammar
would be a device (§ 5.1) that would characteristically perform its role,
but without taking into account the internal organization of strings. Although
such an aim is too narrow, it is interesting to study the various ways in
which the formal devices described in earlier chapters can be put to work
doing just this.

8.1.1
NATURAL LANGUAGES AND
K-LANGUAGES

Even from our present restricted vantage, natural languages can be shown not to be K-languages. If we consider a natural language such as English as a set of sentences without taking into account the way sentences are built, this language cannot be described by a K-grammar or any other equivalent device. Chomsky attempted to prove this statement in the following way.

In a sentence such as

(1) *The rat disappeared,*

we can embed a relative clause, as in

(2) *The rat the cat killed disappeared.*

The process of relative clause attachement is fairly general. Given two sentences that share a common noun phrase (see § 8.4.2.3 below), one of the two *NP*'s can be replaced by a relative pronoun that appears to the left of the remainder of the sentence, and this string is placed to the right of the other *NP* (the antecedent). The relative pronoun has various forms (*who*, *which*, *that*, . . .). In certain cases it can be zeroed, as in (2). Though there are restrictions on the type, place, and role of the *NP* that can be replaced by a relative pronoun, there are few restrictions on the type, place, and role of its antecedent *NP*.[1]

The rules for relative clause embedding are formulated so that they are reapplicable any number of times, and independent of the position of the antecedent. Consequently, a relative clause can be embedded in (2), resulting in

(3) *The rat the cat the dog chased caught disappeared*

and so on. Although it is difficult, if not impossible, to utter or understand sentences such as (3), we must consider them grammatical. They are direct consequences of the formulation of rules. To modify these rules to describe (2) as grammatical, while rejecting (3) as ungrammatical, would be much more complicated and would sacrifice the generality of the formal approach.

In the family of examples we consider, both the main sentence and the

---

[1] The restrictions found are linked to the description of determiners. For example, *president* in *We elected him president* cannot have a relative clause because it cannot have a determiner. The noun *president* in this position cannot be considered a noun phrase.

relative clause have the form

NP V.

The relative pronoun that corresponds to the direct object is zeroed. Then (2) and (3) are represented by the strings $NP^2 V^2$ and $NP^3 V^3$, respectively. Since relative clause embedding can operate any number of times, our family of sentences has the shape

$$R = \{NP^n V^n : n > 0\}.$$

We have shown (§ 6.2.4) that this language is not a K-language, but a C-language (§ 7.2).

We have admitted that sentences R, for $n > 2$, must be considered grammatical, but without explaining why they are unacceptable to native speakers. Certain mechanisms necessary for the perception and actual production of speech set limits on competence, reducing it to the speaker's observed behavior or "performance." We consider competence an infinite automaton of at least the power of p.d.s. automata (since we need at least this type of device to characterize R), but we restrict the corresponding language by an output mechanism with the power of a finite automaton. Under such conditions, strings of R are filtered out for $n > 2$. Notice that this inequality consists in setting an a priori limit ($n = 2$) on the size of the memory tape of a p.d.s. automaton that would characterize R. This argument constitutes a natural description of the set of sentences R actually observed. The argument, however, is incomplete unless we show that R cannot be a subset of some other sublanguage of English that can be generated by a K-grammar. In fact, with our example, if we consider conjunction processes in which *and* is omitted, we have strings such as

John, Paul, Mary left

with subject noun-phrase conjunction, strings such as

The man worked, ate, slept, died

with verb conjunction, and strings such as

John, Paul, Mary worked, ate, slept, died

with both subject noun-phrase and verb conjunction. The set of strings that corresponds to all these constructions is

$$L = \{NP^p V^q : p, q > 0\}$$

We then have $R \subset L$, and L is a K-language.

In other words, it is not true that this type of relative clause self-embedding makes natural languages fall in the class of proper C-languages (i.e., not K-languages). This situation arises because we are only describing strings, and not the interpretations of strings. Thus, sentence (2) is described as one string, regardless of the possible interpretation

The rat and the cat killed and disappeared.

Notice that in the present tense the two interpretations would be written differently:

The rat the cat kills disappears
The rat the cat kill disappear.[2]

Other examples of relative clause embedding show that even on this simplistic descriptive level, natural languages are not K-languages. Presumably, sentences of the same types as the ones just considered, but with the relative pronoun *whom*, constitute a proper C-language of the form

$$R' = \{NP \ (whom \ NP)^m \ V^m \ V: m > 0\}$$

not contained in any K-language part of English. One can show this by considering all places where *whom* is used in English (other types of relative clauses, direct or indirect questions).

8.1.2
NATURAL LANGUAGES AND
C-LANGUAGES

In a similar way, it seems possible to prove that natural languages are not C-languages by showing that there are sublanguages that no C-grammar can describe. Consider the following sentences.

Emeralds and rubies are respectively green and red,
Emeralds, sapphires, and rubies are respectively green, blue, and red.

On each side of *are respectively* are corresponding conjoined strings. When a noun is added on the left, an adjective is added on the right in an unbounded syntactic process. Moreover, nouns and adjectives correspond in a fixed way. By drawing constraints between them, we obtain the pattern of Figure 8.1.

---

[2] We are not concerned with the fact that the two interpretations have different intonation patterns. The actual sentences have pauses either on each side of the relative clause or after each noun and each verb.

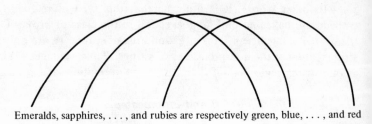

Emeralds, sapphires, . . . , and rubies are respectively green, blue, . . . , and red

FIGURE 8.1

The strings have the shape

$$C = \{N^m \ are \ respectively \ Adj^m : m > 1\}$$

and constitute a C-language. However, if they were described by a C-grammar, the pattern of corresponding constraints would be quite different, the first N corresponding to the last Adj, the second N to the penultimate Adj, and so on, with the last N corresponding to the first Adj. The constraints would be embedded into each other, not cutting across each other, as in our example. C-processes cannot account for the description of such crossing constraints.

In a language such as French, with gender (g) and number (n) agreement between nouns and adjectives of the same sentence, we have a more formal argument: If g and n denote affixes, g can be masculine (g_0) or feminine (g_1) and n can be singular (n_0) or plural (n_1). Our sentences will have shapes similar to

$$Ng_{i_1}n_{i_2} \ Ng_{i_3}n_{i_4} \cdots Ng_i n_{2m-1} \ ^n{}_{i_{2m}} \quad sont \ respectivement$$

$$Adj \ g_{i_1}n_{i_2} \ Adjg_{i_3}n_{i_4} \cdots Adjg_{i_{2m-1}}g_{i_{2m}},$$

where the i's are either 0 or 1. If this family C' of strings (for $m > 1$) were a C-language, any morphic image of it would also be a C-language. Consider the morphism μ defined by

$$g_0 \to a, \ g_1 \to b, \ n_0 \to e, \ n_1 \to e, \ N \to e, \ Adj \to e$$
$$sont \ respectivement \to e.$$

The set $\mu(C') = \{xx : x \in \{a, b\}^* \setminus e\}$ can be shown not to be a C-language. Thus the set of French strings that we considered is not a C-language even on the level of string description independent of the pattern of constraints between N's and Adj's.

8.2

Representation of Constraints

In the examples above we saw that certain sets of sentences could be described on the string level with grammars restricted to a given type. But various inadequacies—inability to properly state certain constraints occurring in these sentences—resulted from the corresponding building processes. It then became necessary to use more powerful grammars.

The sentences $NP^n V^n$ of § 8.1.1 were considered a subset of $NP^p V^q$, and consequently were described by a K-device. But in the linguistic description an important empirical fact was missing. All sentences $NP^n V^n$ are ambiguous in two ways: One interpretation is a sentence with relative clause self-embedding, the other is a sentence with the number of conjoined subjects identical to the number of conjoined verbs. These ambiguities are structural notions that do not appear when we limit descriptions to characteristic devices for strings. If we want to account for ambiguity, we must, for example, describe not only the full set $NP^p V^q$ with a K-grammar but also the set $NP^n V^n$, independently, using a C-grammar. Though sentences with *respectively* can be described on the string level by a C-grammar, if we want to add to the description the constraints actually observed, we need more powerful grammars than C-grammars. Such situations are not uncommon; thus it is interesting to examine the extent to which the formal apparatus for the description of constraints available from definitions of K-grammars and C-grammars is adequate.

8.2.1
TREE STRUCTURES OF K-GRAMMARS

K-rules can also be associated to tree structures, as we did for C-rules (§ 7.3), but their shapes are limited, all being of the type in Figure 8.2. The shape of K-trees immediately shows the limitations of K-grammars. We have recognized, for example, the importance of autonomous structures, such as *NP*, that can recur at various places in a sentence and that make it impossible to state by K-grammar that two *NP*'s appear in the structure of a sentence such as *The man ate the cake*. If this information is to be derived from a state graph, more formal apparatus must be defined.

8.2.2
INADEQUACIES OF C-STRUCTURES

There are also constructions that are difficult to handle with C-rules. Examining conjunction, we observe that all conjoined elements have the

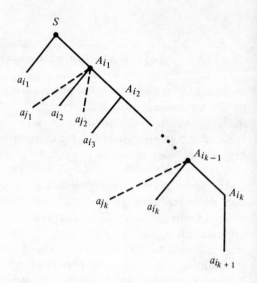

FIGURE 8.2

The a_i's are all terminal. The A_i's are auxiliary symbols. Branching always occurs to the right. The only possible extension consists in allowing more than one terminal symbol to the left of an A_i. The new shapes obtained are indicated with dotted lines; the a_j's correspond to these extra terminal symbols.

same role. A string of conjoined *NP*'s is itself an *NP* and should be represented as in Figure 8.3.

There can be an indefinite number of *NP*'s. But corresponding C-rules have the shape $NP \to (NP)^k$, with fixed k, since the righthand string of a C-rule must have a finite fixed length. A possible solution would be to use a new type of rule, here $NP \to (NP)^*$, that would allow correct representation of conjunctions under the conventions already defined for trees associated to C-rules. An expression such as $NP \to (NP)^*$ holds for an infinite number of

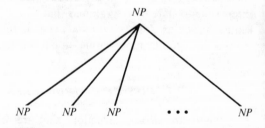

FIGURE 8.3

rules—that is, $NP \to e$, $NP \to NP$, $NP \to NP\,NP$, ..., $NP \to NP^k$, and so on—and has been called a rule schema (§ 3.1.4).

Since K-grammars cannot indicate constituent structure, C-grammars seem to be more adequate, allowing rules such as $S \to NP\,VP$ and $VP \to V\,NP$ (or alternatively the rule $S \to NP\,V\,NP$) to indicate that subjects and direct objects of transitive verbs have the same content, the constituent NP. Such rules, however, are not completely adequate, because they do not account for person-number agreement between subjects and verbs. The rules we mention allow strings such as

John eats cakes

and

The men eats cakes

—both ungrammatical. To prevent their being generated, we have to sub-categorize NP's and V's and to adopt a set of rules such as

$S \to NPsing\ VPsing$

$S \to NPplur\ VPplur,$

where *NPsing* (singular *NP*), *NPplur* (plural *NP*), *VPsing*, and *VPplur* are entirely new auxiliary symbols. We also need

$VPsing \to Vsing\ NP$

$VPplur \to Vplur\ NP,$

where NP is unaltered since verbs and direct objects do not interact.[3]

We are now using three symbols, *NPsing*, *NPplur*, and *NP*, all unrelated except that they belong to V_A. To describe subject-verb agreement by C-rules, we must increase the number of rules[4] and abandon the generalization we tried to capture in giving identical names to the nominal structures in subject and complement positions. If we include in our description features

---

[3] We could dispense with the symbol *NP*, but then, instead of these two rules, we would have to use the four rules

$VPsing \to Vsing\ NPsing,$ $VPsing \to Vsing\ NPplur,$
$VPplur \to Vplur\ NPsing,$ $VPplur \to Vplur\ NPlur,$

which is a less economical solution.

[4] Other rules: $NPsing \to Detsing\ Nsing, \ldots, NP \to Detplur\ Nplur$ are needed to expand the various types of noun phrases.

such as class constraints between subject and verb, and between verb and complement, with notions such as "human" (*hum*) and "nonhuman" (∼*hum*), we must also create the new symbols *NPsing hum, NPsing ∼hum, . . .* for subject positions, and *NP hum, NP ∼hum* for complement positions. We increase considerably the number of rules, only to find that the former rules have all become inadequate. The new grammar cannot be considered an extension of the previous one with the mere addition of rules. The full set of rules must be changed, a defect already observed in finite-state graphs (§ 6.7).

A remedy consists in using new types of rules, which we shall now consider.

8.3

Context-sensitive Languages

8.3.1
DEFINITIONS

Given an auxiliary vocabulary V_A and a terminal vocabulary V_T, rules of the form

$$\alpha A \beta \to \alpha \omega \beta \quad A \in V_A; \quad \alpha, \beta, \omega \in (V_A \cup V_T)^*$$

are called context-sensitive rules. Context-sensitive languages are defined with a finite set of such rules, and an axiom chosen in V_A. We also write

$$A \to \omega; \quad \alpha \overline{\quad\quad} \beta$$

to be read as: The single auxiliary symbol A is rewritten ω in the left context α and in the right context β. If $\alpha = e$, for example, we write $A \to \omega: \overline{\quad\quad}\beta$. C-rules are special cases of context-sensitive rules, with $\alpha = \beta = e$.

The main motivation for using context-sensitive rules is the treatment of the phenomena of subcategorization. Returning to the problems of agreement raised in § 8.2.2, we indicate how context-sensitive rules can provide a solution. First, C-rules provide the general structure:

$$S \to NP\ VP$$

$$VP \to V\ NP$$

$$NP \to Det\ N.$$

Two C-rules will determine the number of each N:

$N \twoheadrightarrow Nsing$

$N \twoheadrightarrow Nplur.$

Once the corresponding derivations are performed, the agreement between subject and verb is stated with context-sensitive rules[5]:

$V \twoheadrightarrow Vsing$; $Nsing$ ——

$V \twoheadrightarrow Vplur$; $Nplur$ ——.

In this way the general distribution of NP's is accounted for, independently of subcategorization. To refine the classification of nouns and verbs, and describe their constraints, only part of the grammar has to be modified; the main structure is left unchanged.

In phonology many phenomena require the use of context-sensitive rules. We mentioned rules that change final s to $/s/$ or $/z/$ depending on the class of consonants C_1 ($/p/$, $/t/$, $/k/$, . . .) or C_2 ($/b/$, $/d/$, $/g/$, . . .) that precedes it. The corresponding rules are

$$C_1 s \rightarrow C_1 /s/ \quad \text{and} \quad C_2 s \rightarrow C_2 /z/.$$

8.3.2
OTHER FORMS OF RULES

8.3.2.1
LENGTH-INCREASING RULES

Rewriting rules such as

(R) $AB \rightarrow BA$

can be interpreted as permuting the two symbols A and B in the course of a derivation. Such rules, though not context-sensitive by our definition, can be replaced by a set of other rules that are context-sensitive and that have exactly the same effect. Suppose that rule (R) belongs to a grammar (G) and consider a new auxiliary symbol M (i.e., $M \notin V_A$). The three rules

$AB \rightarrow AM$ (i.e., $B \rightarrow M$; A ——),

$AM \rightarrow BM$ (i.e., $A \rightarrow B$; ——M),

$BM \rightarrow BA$ (i.e., $M \rightarrow A$; B ——)

are context-sensitive and equivalent to the rule (R).

---

[5] In the same way, determiners are made to agree by the rules *Det Nsing* $\rightarrow$ *Detsing Nsing* and *Det Nplur* $\rightarrow$ *Detplur Nplur*.

More generally, it is possible to replace any rule of the type $\varphi \rightarrow \psi$, $d^0(\varphi) \leqslant d^0(\psi)$, by a sequence of equivalent context-sensitive rules (i.e., the languages generated in the two different ways are identical). As an example of a replacement procedure easily generalized to any rule, we substitute a set of four context-sensitive rules for the rule $A_1 A_2 \rightarrow B_1 B_2 B_3 B_4$ of the above type. We introduce two new auxiliary symbols M_1 and M_2, and we replace the rule by the sequence of context-sensitive rules:

$$A_1 A_2 \rightarrow A_1 M_1, \quad A_1 M_1 \rightarrow M_2 M_1,$$

$$M_2 M_1 \rightarrow B_1 M_1, \quad B_1 M_1 \rightarrow B_1 B_2 B_3 B_4.$$

Consequently, grammars with rules $\varphi \rightarrow \psi$, and φ not longer than ψ, will also be called context-sensitive grammars.

EXAMPLE
_____

$$V_A = \{S, B\}, \qquad V_T = \{a, b\}$$

(1) $S \rightarrow aSBa$

(2) $S \rightarrow aba$

(3) $aB \rightarrow Ba$

(4) $bB \rightarrow bb$

This grammar generates the language $\{a^n b^n a^n : n > 0\}$, which has been noticed not to be a C-language (§ 7.6). Rules (1) and (2) generate strings of the form

$$a^n ba(Ba)^{n-1}, \quad n > 0.$$

Rule (3) operates on them, simultaneously permuting all a's to the right, and all B's next to b. Then rule (4) rewrites all B's as b's. The context guarantees that rule (3) has been applied as many times as possible, insuring that all B's become terminal.

8.3.2.2
SIMULTANEOUS APPLICATIONS OF RULES

Consider the following example, with the rules

(1) $A \rightarrow B; C \underline{\quad\quad} D$

(2) $D \rightarrow E; A \underline{\quad\quad} F$

$\qquad A, B, C, D, E, F \in V_A$

We want to apply them to the sequence $CADF$, a sequence such that either rule (1) or rule (2) can apply, yielding, respectively,

   CBDF and *CAEF*.

When one of the two rules has been applied, the other can no longer apply, since the necessary context has been modified. We could consider "simultaneous" applications of rules instead of our previous sequential applications. Since the sequence $CADF$ is compatible with the two rules, we will apply them simultaneously, and the result will be

   CBEF

—unattainable by sequential application of the two rules. This convention, motivated by empirical findings in phonology, has been shown[6] necessary to obtain the greatest generality in the description of certain phenomena.

8.3.3
FORMAL PROPERTIES

Since context-sensitive rules never shorten strings in a derivation, there is a mechanical procedure for deciding whether or not a given string f belongs to the language of a given grammar. One need only perform all derivations that produce strings of length $d^0(f)$. Since there are a finite number of them, it is easy to check for the presence of f in the set of the derived strings. Context-sensitive languages are thus recursive languages. It can be shown, however, that there are recursive languages that are not context-sensitive.

The class of context-sensitive languages is closed under the operations of union, intersection, complementation, product, reflection, and star. A special type of automaton called a linear bounded automaton characterizes the family of context-sensitive languages. A central unit with a finite number of states directs a reading-writing head that can move a tape in both directions, and can replace any symbol on it by any other symbol including the blank #. Its instructions are identical to Turing-machine instructions, but the amount of tape that can be used in a computation is limited. Given an input of length k (counted in number of squares), the automaton must use an amount of tape that is a linear function of k (i.e., $mk + n$, where m and n are fixed numbers attached to the automaton) (Kuroda). Nondeterministic linear bounded automata are equivalent to context-sensitive grammars. It is not known whether nondeterministic and deterministic linear bounded automata are equivalent.

[6] N. Chomsky and M. Halle, *The Sound pattern of English* (New York: Harper & Row, Publishers, 1968).

8.3.4
APPLICATIONS

We have encountered different examples of analysis performed in terms of contexts, and these motivated the formal definition of context-sensitive grammars. We will now examine the empirical bases of various related devices. In most cases, formalization does not lead to mathematical studies, but has wide application in the statement of rules.

8.3.4.1
COMPLEMENTARY DISTRIBUTIONS

Suppose that, with respect to some linguistic observations, a set of contexts $C = \{x_i\text{———}y_i: 1 \leqslant i \leqslant m\}$ constitutes an interesting class—that, for example, there is a certain wide category $A = \{a_j: 1 \leqslant j \leqslant n\}$ of morphemes, or phonemes, or strings of them, such that the strings $x_i a_j y_i$ are grammatical for all i and j, and ungrammatical for any other context. Now suppose that a certain element b occurs only in a set of contexts $M \subset C$ and that an element c occurs only in the set of contexts $C \setminus M$, the complement set of M with respect to C. The behavior of the elements b and c is exceptional if compared with the one of the a_j's; b and c are said to occur in complementary distribution.

To say that b and c are two forms of some more regular single unit is a generalization about the studied language. Such a statement may take various forms—for example,

$$b \in A, b \to c, \quad \text{in the contexts } C \setminus M,$$

or else

$$c \in A, c \to b, \quad \text{in the contexts } M,$$

or a third solution, consisting in setting up an abstract element $a \in A$, which is regular, and two rules:

$$a \to b \quad \text{in the contexts } M$$
$$a \to c \quad \text{in the contexts } C \,/\, M.$$

The choice of one of these types of solutions depends on both the linguistic data and the theoretical attitude maintained toward linguistic descriptions. We have a clear example with the conjugation of English verbs. If we study the set of English verbs in past forms, we observe that for the large majority of them the past form (V-ed) occurs in the set of contexts

$$C = \{They\text{———}X, They \; have\text{———}X\},$$

where X stands for a sequence of possible complements. For example, *They laughed* and *They have laughed* are grammatical forms; so are *They went* and *They have gone*; but we also have **They gone X* and **They have went X*, whatever X.

The description is the following.

1. The majority of past forms is of the type *V-ed*, and constitutes the set A.
2. The rules

$$go\text{-}ed \rightarrow went; \quad they \text{ ———}$$
$$go\text{-}ed \rightarrow gone; \quad have \text{ ———}$$

account for the situation. The abstract form *go-ed* belongs to A, and is rewritten according to its left context.

In fact, the notion of complementary distributions is much broader than presented here, and the conditions under which forms (there can be more than two) are said to be in complementary distribution are difficult to formalize. This notion, however, is used frequently and constitutes a tool in linguistic research.

8.3.4.2
NOTATIONS FOR RELATED RULES

Notational conventions are used in linguistics to condense related sets of strings that occur in stating a family of rules. For example, if X, Y, and Z represent sets of strings, it is common to write $X(Y)$ for the set $XY \cup X$ (i.e., X with optional Y to the right). The set $XY \cup XZ$ can be written

$$X \left\{ \begin{matrix} Y \\ Z \end{matrix} \right\}.$$

The set $X \cup XY \cup XZ$ can be written either

$$(E_1): \quad X\left(\left\{ \begin{matrix} Y \\ Z \end{matrix} \right\}\right) \qquad \text{or} \qquad (E_2): \quad X\left\{ \begin{matrix} Y \\ (Z) \end{matrix} \right\}$$

—expressions combining both notations. In terms of the polynomial notation, the three preceding sets would be written, respectively,

$$X(e + Y), \qquad X(Y + Z), \quad \text{and} \quad X(e + Y + Z).$$

The parentheses and braces notations are used in syntax and phonology to regroup right members of rules that have the same left member and that correspond to a single linguistic phenomenon. They are also used to condense different contexts in which a given rule may apply. In generative grammar, the meaning of these two notations is more specific, and ordering of the strings entering these expressions is imposed on them. An expression such as $X(Y)$ corresponds to XY and X. When these two ordered elements occur in the statement of a family of rules, the rules that correspond to XY and X are mutually exclusive, at most one of them being applicable. Further, the rule containing XY is applied before the one containing X. Such ordering is said to be disjunctive.

XY and XZ correspond to the expression $X\begin{Bmatrix} Y \\ Z \end{Bmatrix}$. The rules that correspond to XY and XZ apply in this order but do not exclude each other. This ordering is called conjunctive.

With this new interpretation, the expressions (E_1) and (E_2) above are no longer equivalent. In (E_1), X and the pair XY, XZ exclude each other, while in (E_2), X and XZ exclude each other.

Such notations can be translated into polynomial notation. For example, $X\begin{Bmatrix} Y \\ Z \end{Bmatrix}$ can be written $X(Y + Z)$, where the plus sign represents a noncommutative sum. Disjunctive ordering is indicated by the different sign $\oplus$; $X(Y)$ would thus be written $X(Y \oplus e)$, the operation being noncommutative too.

Expressions using braces and parentheses are more powerful than the algebraic notation. Thus the expressions

$$(E_2'): \quad X\begin{Bmatrix} (Y) \\ Z \end{Bmatrix}, \qquad (E_2''): \quad X\begin{Bmatrix} (Y) \\ (Z) \end{Bmatrix}$$

also represent the set of strings $X \cup XY \cup XZ$. Only empirical considerations can determine a choice between both types of devices.

8.3.4.3
AN EXAMPLE OF RULE ORDERING

Let us look at the problem of subcategorizing verbs according to the number and shape of the complements they take. Consider the following structures.

NP V	(intransitive verbs)
NP V NP	(verbs with direct object)
NP V NP prep NP	(verbs with both a direct object and a prepositional complement).

The context-sensitive rules for placing the verbs according to the structures they can enter have the shape

$V \rightarrow$ *gave, showed, . . . ;*   ——— *NP prep NP*
$V \rightarrow$ *ate, beated, . . . ;*   ——— *NP*
$V \rightarrow$ *fell, . . .*

If we now look at a string such as *NP V NP prep NP*, the three preceding types of rules may a priori apply.

1. $V \rightarrow$ *fell*, since it does not need any context.
2. $V \rightarrow$ *ate*, since it applies in the context———*NP*, which is a sub-context of———*NP prep NP*.
3. $V \rightarrow$ *gave* applies according to the full context. Thus, we will get strings such as

These people gave a cake to Paul
*These people ate a cake to Paul
*These people fell a cake to Paul.

A solution that avoids deriving the preceding ungrammatical strings orders the rules from top to bottom as follows.

$V \rightarrow$ *gave;*   ——— *NP prep NP*

$V \rightarrow$ *ate;*   ——— *NP*

$V \rightarrow$ *fell*

and applies them in this order. Once a rule has applied in a given structure, no other rule is applicable to it—a case of disjunctive ordering.

In most cases where this solution can be adopted, it is also possible to use a description that does not involve ordering. For example, by using the boundary symbol ⧺ in the definition of the contexts, the three preceding rules become

$V \rightarrow$ *gave;*   ——— *NP prep NP* ⧺

$V \rightarrow$ *ate;*   ——— *NP* ⧺

$V \rightarrow$ *fell;*   ——— ⧺

and do not have to be ordered, to be applied correctly.

8.4

Transformational Grammars

Though each of the formal devices we presented reflects an aspect of linguistic structure, all of them fail to capture certain linguistically important features. We will indicate what types of data require the use of new forms of rules, and how the mechanisms we have studied are presently integrated in linguistic descriptions.

8.4.1
INADEQUACIES OF CONSTITUENT STRUCTURE

The various formal devices we have presented are, in a way, instances of a single building process: insertion. All the formal rules we have studied perform the same operation: They substitute a string for a name inside a string. Their differences lie in the conditions under which the substitution operates. This restricted range of building processes for strings has been found relevant to the description of natural and artificial languages. Many linguistic phenomena, however, remain unaccounted for by such means. We will consider the most important ones, those that historically led to a radical change in the linguist's views of the structure of natural languages. They were the main cause of the change from phrase-structure models to transformational models.

8.4.1.1
Discontinuous Constituents

A whole class of observations are of the following type. A sentence is analyzed, for example, as

$$u \, a \, v \, c \, b \, w \, X,$$

where u, a, v, b, and c have names that correspond to families of strings, and X is a variable. There is a constraint between u and v that crosses another constraint between a and b. Such facts suggest that u and v on the one hand, a and b on the other, ought to be placed simultaneously in the sentences, though this is not directly possible with the insertion rules we have been using. Examples of such situations are found with agreement phenomena.

In many familiar language, the *NP* subject imposes a person-number affix *pn* to the right of the verb *V* or its tense auxiliary (*Aux*); in the same way, a past-tense auxiliary imposes an ending *-ed* on the right of the verb. The sentence

Mary has chased a boy

is analyzed:

Mary	ha	-s	chas	-ed	a boy
NP	Aux	-pn	V	-ed	NP
u	a	v	c	b	X

The pairs (*NP, -pn*) and (*Aux, -ed*) ought to be described as single units.

Nouns impose upon their determiners a number, and sometimes a gender suffix. In languages such as German and Russian a preposition (left of a noun) is paired with the case suffix of the noun. In such examples, the pairs (determiner, gender-number suffix), (preposition, case suffix), (subject, person-number affix), (auxiliary, tense suffix) behave as single units. However, since their elements, called discontinuous units, are generally separated by some independently constrained segment, they cannot be naturally described by phrase-structure rules.

The transformational approach consists in setting up a basic structure that is generally an abstract form, and as such corresponds to an ungrammatical string of terminal units. A rule will apply to this basic structure that will derive the observed form. In our examples, the basic form will be

$$*u\,v\,a\,b\,c\,X \qquad (NP\text{-}pn\ Aux\text{-}ed\ V\ NP),$$

where, for example, *uv* is introduced by the phrase-structure rule $U \rightarrow uv$, and *ab* by $A \rightarrow ab$. The transformation rules will be of the type

(P) $u\,v\,a \rightarrow u\,a\,v$ (*NP-pn Aux* → *NP Aux-pn*)

(Q) $a\,b\,c \rightarrow a\,c\,b$ (*Aux-ed V* → *Aux V-ed*)

(P) permutes *v* and *a* and (Q) permutes *b* and *c*, thus providing the grammatical string *uavcbwX*. Notice that rule (Q) must apply before rule (P). Although these rules are equivalent to context-sensitive rules, we consider them a different type, since context-sensitive rules do not reflect the permutation process needed here.

8.4.1.2
TRANSFORMATIONAL RELATIONS

Another type of linguistic phenomenon requires rules different from substitution procedures. If we consider pairs of sentences such as

(1) *John examined the situation*
(2) *The situation was examined by John*

and if we insist on restricting ourselves to phrase-structure rules for grammatical description, we are forced to use for them a set of rules such as

   (i) $S \to NP\ VP$ common to (1) and (2)

   (ii) $VP \to V\ NP$ for (1)

   (iii) $VP \to V'\ prep\ NP$ for (2).

Then, except that both (1) and (2) (as do most sentences) have a subject and a predicate [rule (i)], the two sentences are derivationally unrelated. In the description of English, they are no more related than the sentences

The bullet hit the car

and

John was sentenced by mistake[7]

which have structures (i.e., patterns of subject, auxiliary, verb, and complement) similar to those of (1) and (2), respectively. Such a description ignores an important observation.

Let us consider all the sentences of English that can be analyzed as

   NP V NP (X).

The *NP* to the right of *V* is a direct object, defined by the possibility of substituting for it one of the pronouns *them, him, her, it*; *X* is a variable ranging over other possible complements.

If we study the lexicon of English, we can make a list of verbs that can have a direct object in the preceding sense. It is an empirical fact that whenever a verb has a direct object, it also enters a construction of the type of (2) (i.e., a passive construction). Then, the direct object becomes the subject, the subject becoming a complement preceded by the preposition *by*, and the

---

[7] Notice that this sentence is not the passive form of *Mistake sentenced John* but rather of a sentence such as *Someone sentenced John by mistake*, with the undetermined agent *by someone* omitted.

same verb V occurs in the special form V': auxiliary *to be* followed by the past participle of V. More precisely, whenever a verb V enters the "active" construction

(A) *NP V^t NP (X)*

(V^t indicates V is in tense t, the second *NP* is the direct object), in general it also enters the "passive" construction

(P) *NP be^t V-ed NP (X)*.

With respect to (A), the two *NP*'s have been interchanged; *V-ed* is read "past participle form of V." The form *V-ed* can involve the affix *-en* instead of *-ed* as in *eaten*, and/or changes in the root V, as in *read, thought, broken*, and so on.

Examination of the classes of nouns that occur as main nouns in the *NP*'s of (A) and (P) shows that the classes allowed in subject positions of (A) are the classes allowed in the *NP* preceded by *by* in (P), and that the classes of the direct objects of (A) are the classes found as subjects of (P). Moreover, when a noun raises some question of acceptability in (A) [as in (*sincerity* + *science*) *examined Paul*], exactly the same peculiarity is found in the corresponding (P) [*Paul was examined by* (*sincerity* + *science*)]. All these observations constitute an important regularity that must be accounted for. A natural way of doing it is by stating a passive transformation between (A) and (P), a rule such that

NP V^t NP (X) → *NP be^t V-ed by NP (X)*,

where the arrow has the usual meaning "is rewritten," and the various symbols are as defined above. We will discuss later the meaning of such a rule.

8.4.2
FORMALIZATION
OF TRANSFORMATIONS

More examples of inadequate descriptions could be given, and in many cases a natural solution to the difficulty consists in using a new type of rule with a more complex effect than substitution. The exact form of these rules is still a subject of much linguistic research, but certain features suggest a general framework for formalization.

8.4.2.1
RULES OF TRANSFORMATIONS

If we return to the passive rule above,

$$NP \; V^t \; NP \; (X) \rightarrow NP \; be^t \; V\text{-}ed \; by \; NP \; (X),$$

and if we apply to it the conventions of rewriting rules, it also reads

$$V^t \rightarrow be^t \; V\text{-}ed \; by; \qquad NP \;\text{------}\; NP \; (X)$$

(i.e., the verb is replaced by a slightly different verbal expression in a given context that is left unchanged). The reading of the rule would provide "passive" strings such as *John was examined by the situation* from (1) above, which is undesirable. We must state explicitly that the two *NP*'s exchange their positions. We will then associate with each transformable string an index, by numbering in increasing order and from left to right (i.e., by naming) the elements to be transformed. The result of the transformation is described by the elements of the index. The passive rule is then approximately written:[8]

$$NP \; V^t \; NP \; (X)$$

$$1 \quad 2 \quad 3 \quad 4 \;\; \rightarrow \; 3 \; be^t \; 2\text{-}ed \; by \; 1 \; 4.$$

The left member of such a rule is called an *analysis* of the sentence (or part of it) to be transformed. Here we use one of the possible analyses of active sentences that could also be analyzed as

$$NP \; VP$$

$$1 \quad 2$$

but this analysis is not relevant to the passive form.

In the same way, the rule (P) used for discontinuous segments (§ 8.4.1.1) could read

$$v \; a \rightarrow a \; v; \qquad u \;\text{------}.$$

---

[8] We should in fact further analyze V^t (and be^t) into a verbal root V found in each member of the rule, and a tense, which can be either a suffix alone or a discontinuous pair (auxiliary, suffix), as we outlined in § 8.4.1.1.

Although it is not ambiguous as with the passive, we write

$u\,v\,a \rightarrow$

1 2 3

1 3 2,

making the permutation explicit.

The effect of transformations is complex. They operate, indeed, on treelike structures. This appears clearly in the case of the passive. In general, the passive rule operates independently of the content of the subject *NP* and the direct object *NP*. These two *NP*'s can in fact be very complex structures. Since the rule only mentions *NP*'s, and does not refer to their content, it is quite general. Further, the result of a transformation must be a treelike structure, since other transformations may operate on it too.

For example, passive sentences may be submitted to the question transformation:

The situation was examined by John
Was the situation examined by John?

We need a treelike structure for passive sentences, which means the passive rule is not limited to shuffling various strings and introducing new material, but it must restructure its result. One possible way of expressing this consists in writing the rule as in Figure 8.4. Such rules are rather removed in formal complexity from the simple rewriting rules we defined on strings. These rules are not building rules, and do not introduce progressively various

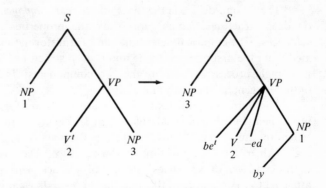

FIGURE 8.4

The rule is defined on the minimal subtree needed for the passive. In a sentence, there can be other parts that are unaffected by the transformation.

elements of a sentence, starting from an axiom, but are operators that act on sentences already built, modifying them in complicated ways.

8.4.2.2
ORGANIZATION OF A GRAMMAR

A transformational generative grammar is organized in the following way. A first device called the *base component* generates basic or deep structures from the axiom by a system of C-rules and context-sensitive rules. Deep structures, constructs that are remote from observed sentences, are justified on various grounds. They must be as simple as possible, and there should be only a small number of elementary types of such structures. The transformations that act on them should be as general as possible and should explain the numerous apparent irregularities observed in actual sentences. The C-rules are thus as limited as possible in number and type. They consist mainly of the rule types

$$
\begin{aligned}
S &= \#NPVP\#^9 \\
VP &= V(E + NP)\,(E + prepNP) \\
NP &= Det\ N\ that\ S.
\end{aligned}
$$

The symbols $\#$ are sentence boundaries.

The use of context-sensitive rules is restricted to subcategorization and lexical insertion in the mode exemplified in § 8.3.4.3 above. Deep structures contain all of the information necessary to build and to understand the corresponding sentences.

The second device is the *transformational component*. Its rules operate on deep structures, which possess all the properties observed in actual sentences. The empirical determination of transformations cannot be separated from the assumptions made about deep structures. For linguists, there is a single process in building the two components. The results should be optimally general, natural, and simple.

The third component has the surface structures for input, and it interprets them by phonological rules. The lexical items introduced into deep structures are abstract forms modified by the *phonological component* according to their syntactic position in the sentence. The outputs are phonetic representations of sentences, strings of phones with physical properties attached to them that resemble in different respects what is heard (or uttered) by the speakers of the language.

---

[9] The introduction of the symbol *VP* can perhaps be motivated on a level of rather superficial observation. It is unclear whether it should be used in deep structures, or reserved to make explicit a surface property.

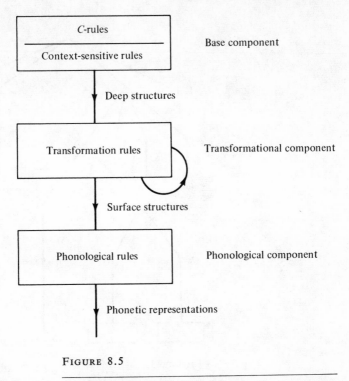

FIGURE 8.5

The arrows indicate the possible paths in the application of
the rules.

Various hypotheses have been formulated about the shape of a *semantic
component*, but this is a difficult subject and current proposals are still in state
of flux. Nothing precise can be said about it, from a formal point of view.

Many questions arise concerning the application of rules in grammars
of the type shown in Figure 8.5. We will examine a few important features of
the interaction between components.

8.4.2.3
BLOCKING

As an example, we will examine the deep structure corresponding to a relative
clause adjoined to the subject of an intransitive verb. The relative clause has
an intransitive main verb, too. We use the rules

(B)
$$S = \#NP\ VP\#$$
$$VP = V_i$$
$$NP = DetN\ that\ S$$
$$NP = DetN.$$

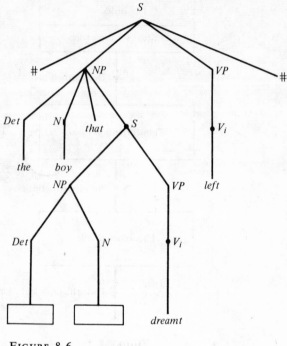

FIGURE 8.6

For the moment, we leave the lexical items of the subject of the relative clause unspecified.

The structure is given in Figure 8.6. Certain lexical rules have been applied, such as

(L) $\quad\begin{array}{l} Det = the + a + some + \cdots \\ N = boy + girl + man + \cdots \\ V_i = dreamt + left + \cdots \end{array}$

This is the basic structure of the sentence

The boy that dreamt left.

It can be derived when the subject of the embedded sentence is *the boy* (i.e., when the two boxes left empty in Figure 8.6 are filled with *the* and *boy*). We have then identity with the antecedent. However, a different situation may arise. Rules (B) and (L) above apply starting from any S; they apply independently to the main S and to the embedded S, and there is no control of the elements of the main *S* over the elements of the embedded *S*. It is possible to derive the structure of Figure 8.6 with *a girl* filling the empty boxes. Since the relative clause transformation only applies when there are two "identical" *NP*'s in a structure, it is not applicable. The rule, among other effects, erases the two nonterminal sentence boundaries ⫫. Consequently, the latter structure cannot produce a terminal string, and the derivation is said to be blocked.

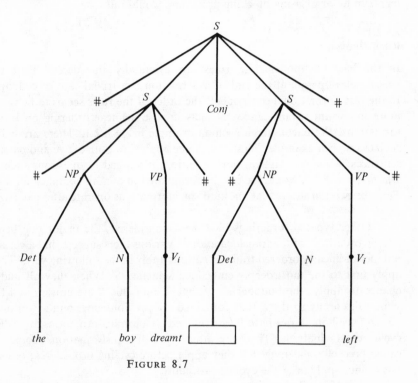

FIGURE 8.7

Grammars allowing this possibility are called *blocking grammars*. It is an empirical question whether or not grammars of natural languages should possess this property. Alternatively one could require that grammars of natural languages be such that all their derivations lead to terminal strings. Relative clause embedding is not an obvious counterexample to such a hypothesis, since the following analysis is quite plausible. The deep structure of the sentence *The boy that dreamt left* could be of the type of Figure 8.7. When the empty boxes are filled by *the girl*, for example, relativization is impossible; the structure is realized as a conjunction of two sentences, the symbol *Conj* becoming the coordinating conjunction *and*. We then have the terminal string *The boy dreamt and the girl left*. When the boxes are filled by *the boy*, we can either have conjunctions such as

the boy dreamt and the boy left   and   *the boy dreamt and left*

or else relativization, in which case *Conj* is realized as a subordinating conjunction (*that*), and the structure of Figure 8.6 is derived from that of Figure 8.7. If such an analysis could be further supported, one of the main arguments in favor of using blocking grammars would fail.

8.4.2.4
RULE ORDERING

In the base component the rules are essentially unordered. That the lexical rules operate at the end of a derivation is a trivial case of ordering. In the transformational component, the order of the rules seems to be much more important. Many empirical facts impose a linear ordering on transformations. We encountered such an example in § 8.4.1.1. There are many such cases. For example, questions can be applied to both active and passive sentences, while the passive transformation, if applied to questions such as *Did they see Bill?*, would have to be formulated in a more complicated way. This observation shows that question transformations operate after passivization.

Other types of orderings have been considered, the major one being "cyclic ordering" of the transformations. Various facts suggest that a certain number of linearly ordered transformations apply in the following way. They apply first to the most deeply embedded sentence *S*. When they all had a chance to apply, the boundaries $\#$ that delimit this *S* are erased, and the same rules apply to the *S* that contained the previous one, and so on until all sentence boundaries have been removed. Such transformations are called cyclic transformations. There are other types of transformations; some are called precyclic, meaning that they apply before cycling procedures; others, postcyclic, apply after the cycling procedures.

These formal properties depend on many unanswered empirical questions, the solution of which may very well lead to some other views about the organization of a grammar.

8.4.2.5
FORMAL PROPERTIES

Transformational grammars can be given various formal definitions under various empirical hypotheses. They can then be investigated mathematically within recursive function theory. It has been shown[10] that under the most interesting hypotheses, transformational grammars generate the

---

[10] P. S. Peters and R. W. Ritchie, "On the Generative Power of Transformational Grammars," *Information and Control* (New York: The Academic Press, 1971).

full class of recursively enumerable languages. The reason is that many linguistic facts must be described by erasing rules (ellipsis). So far no general principle restricting erasing procedures is available that controls the excessive power of transformational grammars and is at the same time empirically adequate.

8.4.3
HARRIS' VIEWS OF
TRANSFORMATIONS

We have presented Chomsky's definitions of a transformational grammar, but there are other views, the most important being Harris' conception.

In Chomsky's generative grammar, transformations are essentially rewriting rules as we defined them in Chapter II; the trees and the index associated with the rules simply make them unambiguous.

For Harris, a transformation is a relation between sentences; much less attention is paid to the arrow that in Chomsky's framework relates a sentence and its transform. Between two transforms S_1 and S_2 Harris writes a double arrow:

$$S_1 \leftrightarrow S_2.$$

A sequence such as

$$P_1 \leftrightarrow P_2 \leftrightarrow \cdots \leftrightarrow P_n$$

is the analog of a derivation; it defines a set of equivalent sentences in which one element is distinguished. The element is usually the simple declarative sentence (with one verb), called a kernel sentence. The orientation of the derivations, essential in Chomsky's generative grammars, is here a simple consequence of the choice of particular structures as kernel sentences. This choice is dictated principally by morphological simplicity.

From a strictly empirical point of view there is little difference between the two conceptions. The main differences lie in certain questions that can be asked about the two formal apparatuses. In fact, a certain equivalence between the two types of systems can be foreseen by analogy to formal systems. We indicated (§ 3.2) that Thue systems (with nonoriented rules—that is, with a double arrow between the two members) were equivalent to semi-Thue systems (where the rules are oriented by a simple arrow). Moreover, Thue systems and algebraic systems are almost identical devices.

The difference between the two types of transformational grammar is to a large extent the one that can be observed between algebraic and semi-Thue rewriting systems. Harris' view is much more algebraic, as his terminology clearly indicates, while Chomsky insists on placing the grammars of natural languages within the framework of formal systems and automata.

To the extent that empirical questions are still crucial to the construction of the formal apparatus, it remains possible for a linguist to neglect the technical differences between Harris' and Chomsky's conceptions.

Conclusion

There is a certain variety in the use of mathematics in the study of natural languages.

The first significant work is Markov's study in 1913 of the statistical distribution of letters in the text of Eugene Onegin. It founded the theory of Markov chains, an important concept in mathematics and physics. Markov determined the frequencies of the letters that appeared to the right of all sequences of k letters ($k = 1, 2, 3, \ldots$) found in the text. These frequencies can, superficially, be considered a model of language. Notice that this study is already "formal" in that it relies only on the occurrences of letters between word boundaries and does not rely on the meaning of the units involved.

The same is true of Shannon's work, though the relevance of his examples to linguistics is rather artificial, and the deep significance of the notion of redundancy he is interested in is to be found within information theory, not natural languages. However, when the structures these scientists defined are limited to their algebraic part, ignoring the probability distributions, they have a much richer meaning for linguistics. They correspond to the finite-state processes (i.e., K-languages).

Another well-known study dealing with probabilities is Zipf's,[1] but his "law" has been found to be of such generality that no precise use of it can be made in linguistics.[2]

None of the notions we have presented here dealt with probabilities or frequencies. What we call mathematical linguistics is a recent field whose birth dates to the 1950's, resulting from cross influences between structural linguistics and other fields.

We have restricted the much broader field of mathematical linguistics to the main notions with immediate empirical relevance. For example, we have not presented the concept of unsolvability (or undecidability). Although it is an important notion in this field, it has no direct empirical interpretation.

No technical mathematical proofs have been given. The few cases where we define abstract algebraic devices are rather removed from everyday linguistic practice. However, these definitions ought to be of a greater interest to mathematicians, since they result from recent and important linguistic studies, and they simultaneously constitute a basis for new mathematical theories that are conceptually related to fields as important as group or number theory.

To reach a stage where subfields of mathematics became meaningful to them, linguists had to modify their attitude toward language and grow more concerned with combinatorial properties of linguistic elements. Under the influence of logic, linguists axiomatized their procedures and followed to the end the consequences of their methods. All this work has allowed a meaningful introduction of mathematical tools in linguistics.

This development, however, should not be compared to the use of mathematical tools in physics. In physics, numerous mathematical models allow pure calculations and mathematical explorations that predict important facts of a strictly physical nature. No such situation can be found today in linguistics (excepting, perhaps, Chomsky's demonstration that natural languages are not finite-state languages). Rather, mathematical tools in linguistics have the status of atomic-particle accelerators in physics. These machines enable physicists to uncover numerous new facts about the nucleus, and thus to question in a very deep (and sometimes unclear) way the nature of the physical universe. Formal methods in linguistics have a similar role. Logical and mathematical concepts such as algebraic and formal systems and automata have enabled linguists to discover many new constraints inside words, and inside sentences, formerly overlooked by grammarians and speakers. They have also allowed specialists to raise new questions about this exceptional apparatus that man puts to use for so many purposes.

---

[1] G. K. Zipf, *The Psychobiology of Language* (Boston: Houghton Mifflin Company, 1935).

[2] B. Mandelbrot, "On the Theory of Word Frequencies and on Related Markovian Models," *Proc. XII Symp. Am. Math. Soc.* (Providence, 1961).

Selected Readings

BAR-HILLEL, Y., *Language and Information; Selected Essays on their Theory and Application*. Jerusalem: Academic Press, Addison-Wesley, 1964.

BRAINERD, B., *Introduction to the Mathematics of Language Study*. New York: American Elsevier Publishing Co., 1971.

CHOMSKY, N. and G. A. MILLER, chaps. 11, 12, and 13 in D. Luce, R. R. Bush, and E. Galanter, eds., *Handbook of Mathematical Psychology*, vol. II. New York: John Wiley & Sons, Inc., 1963.

CHOMSKY, N., *Aspects of the Theory of Syntax*. Cambridge, Mass.: M.I.T. Press, 1964.

DAVIS, M., *Computability and Unsolvability*. New York: McGraw-Hill, Inc., 1958.

GINSBURG, S., *The Mathematical Theory of Context-Free Languages*. New York: McGraw-Hill, Inc., 1966.

GROSS, M., and A. LENTIN, *Introduction to Formal Grammars*, trans. M. Salkoff. Heidelberg and New York: Springer-Verlag, 1970.

HARRIS, Z. S., *Mathematical Structure of Language*. New York: John Wiley & Sons, Inc., 1968.

HOPCROFT, J. E. and J. D. Ullman, *Formal Languages and their Relation to Automata.* Reading, Mass.: Addison-Wesley Publishing Company, Inc., 1969.

KIEFER, F., *Mathematical Linguistics in Eastern Europe.* New York: American Elsevier Publishing Co., 1968.

KURODA, S. -Y., "Classes of Languages and Linear-bounded Automata," *Information and Control*, vol. 7 (1964), pp. 207–223.

MYHILL, J., *Linear-bound Automata*, Tech. note 60-165, Wright Air Develop. Div., 1960.

SCHUTZENBERGER, M.-P., "On a Theorem of R. Jungen," *Proc. Am. Math. Soc.* (1962), pp. 189–197.

WALL, R. E., *Introduction to Mathematical Linguistics.* Englewood Cliffs, N.J.: Prentice-Hall, Inc., 1972 (to appear).

Index

A

Ambiguity, 14, 23, 105, 112, 129
    inherent, 106

B

Blocking, 28, 32, 35, 42, 80, 147, 149, 150

C

C-:
    grammar, 102, 106–16, 118, 120, 122,
      127, 129, 131
    language, 8, 103, 108, 112–14, 118–22,
      126–28
    rule, 102, 107–9, 122, 129–33, 146
Characterization of languages, 29, 32, 34,
    52, 57, 59, 60, 61, 62, 64, 69, 85, 94, 120,
    124

Chevalley, C., 16
Chomsky, N., 5, 25, 105, 116, 125, 135, 151,
    152, 154
Church, A., 6, 35, 52
Competence, 99, 126
Concatenation, 14, 16, 17, 48, 85, 89
Congruence, 47, 48, 50, 51
Conjunction, 2, 3, 5, 21, 63, 68, 73, 74, 97,
    102, 126, 127, 129, 130, 149, 150
Constituent:
    discontinuous, 102, 140, 141, 144
    structure, 100, 108, 109, 110, 131, 140
Constraint, 66, 67, 68, 70, 123, 127, 128,
    129, 132, 133
    finite, 67, 68, 70, 99, 119
    infinite, 67, 70, 119
Context-free:
    grammar (*see* C-grammar)

Context-free: (cont.)
 language, 100 (*see* C-language)
 rule, 102 (*see* C-rule)
Context sensitive:
 grammar, 134, 135, 136
 language, 132, 135
 rule, 132–35, 139, 141, 146

D

Davis, M., 58
Deletion (*see* Zeroing)
Derivation, 38, 39, 42, 45–48, 50, 58, 82–84, 103–9, 112, 118, 133, 135, 148, 149, 151
Deterministic, 29, 31, 94, 116, 135
Dyck language, 120–22

E

Embedding (*see* Self-embedding)
Equation (algebraic), 110, 111

F

Finite automaton (*see* Finite-state automaton)
Finite-state:
 automaton, 78–81, 87–91, 93, 94, 99, 114, 115, 118, 119, 126
 computation, 79–81
 grammar, 82 (*see* K-grammar)
 graph, 81, 83–88, 92, 94–97, 99, 129, 132
 language, 78, 81, 153, 154 (*see* K-language)
Friedman, J., 64

G

Group, 50, 51, 61
 free, 121

H

Halle, M., 25, 135
Harris, Z. S., 5, 24, 76, 151, 152

I

Infinite automaton, 36, 119
Insertion, 21, 22, 39, 50, 51

J

Joshi, A. K., 64

K

K-:
 grammar, 84, 125, 126, 129, 131
 language, 8, 78, 83–85, 87, 93–96, 103, 108, 112, 114, 119, 120, 125–27, 153
 rule, 102, 107
Kleene, S. C., 51, 78
Kuroda, S. Y., 135

L

Linear grammar, 108
Linear-bounded automaton, 135

M

Mandelbrot, B., 154
Markov, A., 6, 59
Markov, A. A., 99, 153
Matthews, G. H., 116
Metalinear grammar, 108
Mirror, 106, 113
Monoid, 15, 16, 50, 62, 91, 92
 finite, 15, 91, 93
 free, 16, 22, 49, 50, 69
Morphism, 12, 13, 23, 49–51, 72, 91, 93, 121–23, 128

N

Nondeterministic, 29, 31, 56, 94, 116, 135
Nesting (*see* Self-embedding)
Normal grammar, 108

P

Performance, 99, 126
Permutation, 44, 75, 77, 133, 141, 145
Peters, P. S., 150
Petrick, S., 64
Phrase structure, 140, 141
Polynomial, 6, 16, 17, 18, 24, 25, 137, 138
Post, E., 46
Power series, 16, 18, 111, 112
Programming language, 7, 8, 35, 108
Push-down storage automaton, 114–16, 118, 119, 126

R

Rabin, M. O., 79
Recursive language, 34, 61, 63–65, 135
Recursively enumerable languages, 34, 53, 61, 63–65, 151
Regular:
    expression, 85, 86
    language, 78 (*see* K-language)
Ritchie, R. W., 150
Rodgers, Jr., Hartley, 6
Ross, J. R., 45
Rule:
    rewriting, 39, 45, 49, 55–58, 73–77, 82, 102, 133, 143, 144
    schema, 44, 131

S

Schützenberger, M. P., 51, 87, 112, 116, 120
Scott, D., 79
Self-embedding, 107, 108, 119, 125–28, 148, 149
Semigroup, 16
Sequential grammar, 108
Shannon, C., 99, 153
Situation, 28, 31, 32, 115
Stage graph (*see* Finite-state graph)
Submonoid, 91
Substitution, 31, 32, 38, 39, 45, 54–56, 60, 61, 96, 100, 102, 104, 142

System:
    algebraic, 46, 51, 62, 87, 120, 122, 151, 152, 154
    combinatorial, 37, 45
    formal, 37, 38, 41–45, 52–54, 56, 58, 69, 83, 151, 152, 154
    normal, 46
    Post, 46
    rewriting, 37, 40, 44, 45, 50–52, 56–65, 72–74, 83, 114, 120, 152
    semi-Thue, 45, 151, 152
    Thue, 45, 46, 151
Star operation, 14–16, 25, 86, 95, 113, 114, 135

T

Thue, 45, 46, 151, 152
Transformation, 1, 39, 44, 77, 141–46, 149, 150
Transformational grammar, 140, 146, 150, 151
Turing Machine, 6, 26–36, 52–63, 65, 69, 74–79, 83, 114, 135
    universal, 35

Z

Zeroing, 50, 54, 74, 125, 151
Zipf, G. K., 154